STORIES OF THE FIRST WORLD WAR

THE MEN, WOMEN, CHILDREN AND ANIMALS THAT PLAYED THEIR PART

NEVER SUCH INNOCENCE

COMMEMORATING THE MEN AND WOMEN OF THE GREAT WAR

A CENTENARY PROJECT

FOREWORD BY DAN SNOW

First published in 2018 by
Never Such Innocence
www.neversuchinnocence.com
Never Such Innocence. Registered Charity Number 1156148

CONTENTS

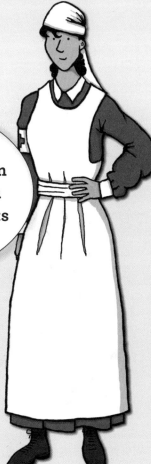

FOREWORD

The First World War was a military, political, economic and human catastrophe which destroyed millions of lives and fundamentally altered the course of human history. It tore up the map of Europe and toppled ancient empires. It left chaos in its wake, revolutions, civil wars, ethnic cleansing and bitterness which meant that the legacy of the war extended far beyond the end of formal hostilities in 1918. In fact we are still living with the consequences of the war. Turmoil in the Middle East, tensions with Russia, ethnic squabbling in Eastern Europe are all symptoms of a world that has still not dealt with the fallout of the war.

As this excellent resource points out, the effects on Britain were just as profound. Hundreds of thousands of men had been killed; many more bore the physical and psychological scars. Britain was victorious but almost bankrupt. There had been great changes to society. Women had challenged how they were seen by successfully taking on jobs that had supposedly been the exclusive preserve of men. After the war many women were given the vote for the first time to reflect their contribution, and millions of working class men were also given the vote as returning soldiers and workers in key war industries demanded a greater say in how the country was run. Britain entered the democratic era as a result of the war. This new electorate was more interested in rebuilding their country and spending Government money on welfare than on more battleships.

The war changed Britain and the world. Only by understanding it and its consequences can we make sense of the world around us today. This resource produced by Never Such Innocence gives us an excellent account of the war, its effect on society, art and culture. It is a great place for young people to start learning and engaging with our shared history.

DAN SNOW – *HISTORIAN*

Editor: Lucy Kentish
Research: Lucy Kentish, Maddie Messenger, Eleanor Stephens
Illustrations: Dan Hinge
Initial design: Elly Preston
Design: Damian Jaques
Production: Mark Fletcher

Never Such Innocence would also like to thank the following people and organisations for their kind contribution to and assistance with the making of this book:

Air Historical Branch
An Lanntair
Megan Barrett
Daniel Barry
Matthieu Baumgartner
Lynette Beardwood
Mel Bradley
Kate Brett
Britannica Digital Learning
Cavell Nurses Trust
The Cartoon Museum
Changing Faces
Combat Stress
Commonwealth War Graves Commission
Sebastian Cox
The Curzon Institute
Dr Santanu Das
Dan Dayton
Katherine Diamond
Joke Dieryckx
Boris Dralyuk
English Heritage
Far From the Western Front
First Aid Nursing Yeomanry
Great War Africa Association
Professor Laurence Grove
Eleanor Harding
Historical Association
Imperial War Museum
Francis Ledwidge Museum
Paula Kitching
Dr Megan Leyland
Alan Lywd
Dr Edward Madigan
Tom McGarry
Jan Melichar
Dr Dan Mulhall

National Army Museum
Naval Historical Branch
Dr Vivien Newman
New Zealand High Commission
Dr Jennifer Novotny
Harry Oates
Dr John Patterson
Peace Pledge Union
Katya Rogatchevskaia
The Royal British Legion
Dr Anne Samson
Professor Ingrid Sharp
Dr Gary Sheffield
Dan Snow
Snowdonia National Park
Jack Sowry
Dr Martin Stephen
Professor David Stevenson
Sir Hew Strachan DL
Marianne Taylor
Matthew Tonks
Nathalie Trouveroy
Alison Truphet
Lukas Van Damme
Volksbund Deutsche Kriegsgräberfürsorge
Prof Vlasis Vlasidis
Mark Warby
We Were There Too: London Jews in the First World War
Caroline Wilkes
Yasmin Winsdale
World War One Centennial Commission
WW100 Scotland
WW100 New Zealand
13 Hundred Creative Partners
14-18 NOW

INTRODUCTION

Inspiration for this book came from a First World War centenary project, Never Such Innocence (NSI). The charity takes its name from a line in Philip Larkin's poem MCMXIV, which reflects on the immense changes caused by the First World War.

This book was compiled over four years and provides the opportunity to reflect on our shared history.

NSI worked with Embassies, High Commissions and historians internationally to explore different stages of the war and offer a broad range of perspectives and experiences from the period. Subjects featured include major battles, the war in the skies and at sea, spies, cartoons, objections to war, women at the front, animals, and sports at war. The chapters have poetry and art from the war period incorporated throughout to inspire readers to create their own poetry, art or songs.

This unique cross-curricular resource may be used at home or in school to inspire and inform you about the First World War. We have created

characters to guide you through your journey. Join Munitionette Molly, Flight Lieutenant Hew, Sepoy Joti and their friends as you learn about this period of history that changed the world.

Alongside this book, NSI ran an international creative arts competition for each year of the centenary to enable young people to play their part in the commemorations. The competition invited 9 to 16 year olds to submit poetry, art or songs inspired by the events of the war. All of the winning entries from the four centenary competitions have been published in an anthology, *Never Such Innocence: Children's Responses through Poetry, Art and Song*.

Use this book and the anthology to inspire your own centenary legacy.

My name is Fifi and this is my friend Gaston...

We're here to give you an insight into life on the front line.

THE OUTBREAK OF WAR

In the years leading up to the First World War, Germany sought to gain international presence by extending her empire and increasing her naval capacity.

Germany, Austria-Hungary and Italy formed the Triple Alliance in 1882, agreeing to support each other if attacked by either France or Russia. The objective of the Anglo-French Entente Cordiale of 1904 was to settle Britain and France's disagreements outside Europe, in Africa and Asia. France and Russia had an alliance from 1894, and in 1907 Russia and Britain reached agreements about Central Asia. These agreements gradually developed to form the Triple Entente, from 1905-07 onwards the three countries were co-operating more closely against Germany.

When **Archduke Franz Ferdinand**, heir to the throne of Austria-Hungary, was assassinated in Bosnia-Herzegovina in June 1914 (see box), the **Austro-Hungarians issued an ultimatum to Serbia** which would make Serbia an effective client-state of the Austrians. It was expected that Serbia would reject the ultimatum, providing a pretext for a war against them, but running the risk of drawing Russia in on the side of Serbia. With this in mind, Austria-Hungary sought assurances from Germany that she would come to her aid if Russia declared war in support of Serbia.

Dissatisfied with Serbia's response, Austria-Hungary declared war on 28th July. This sparked a series of events that culminated in the Great War. Russia announced the mobilisation of her army, which Germany viewed as a threat to the Austrians and to themselves, and thus declared war on Russia and its ally France on 1st and 3rd August, respectively.

Britain had initially hoped for a diplomatic solution to the situation; she feared that if Germany were to defeat France, Europe would be dominated by a single, militarist autocracy. Germany launched her attack on France on 4th August, invading neutral Belgium in an attempt to bypass French defences. The Germans aimed to defeat France before turning eastward to Russia.

This act of war broke the **1839 Treaty of London**, which committed all the major European powers, including Britain and Germany, to guard the neutrality of Belgium. Britain was nervous that a German success against Belgium or France would guarantee German domination of Europe, and particularly the northwest coast facing Britain, and so presented an ultimatum to Germany.

ASSASSINATED

On 28th June 1914, Archduke Franz Ferdinand, heir to the throne of the Austro-Hungarian Empire, was assassinated. The Archduke and his wife were shot by Gavrilo Princip, a member of the Black Hand Gang, an organisation that wanted to rid Bosnia of Austrian rule, while they were visiting Sarajevo, Bosnia. Shortly afterwards, Austria-Hungary declared war on Serbia, and the chain of events that led to the First World War was set in motion.

GERMAN PLANNING

THE GERMAN GENERAL STAFF PREPARED PLANS ON ANNUAL CYCLE. IT FACED RUSSIA TO ITS EAST AND FRANCE TO ITS WEST, AND ITS PLANS INCLUDED WAR WITH EACH OF THEM OR BOTH AT THE SAME TIME. FROM 1892 THE CHIEF OF THE GENERAL STAFF, ALFRED VON SCHLIEFFEN PRIORITISED THE WAR AGAINST FRANCE AS IT WAS EASIER TO INVADE QUICKLY, AND HIS SUCCESSOR, HELMUTH VON MOLTKE, STAYED WITH THAT PRIORITY UP TO 1914.

THE STRENGTH OF THE FRANCO–RUSSIAN ALLIANCE MEANT THAT WAR WITH ONE WAS LIKELY TO MEAN WAR WITH THE OTHER. THE PLAN RESTED ON THE HOPE THAT FRANCE COULD BE BEATEN QUICKLY, AND THAT RUSSIA WOULD TAKE SIX WEEKS TO MOBILISE ITS ARMY.

RUSSIA ISSUED ITS ORDER FOR GENERAL MOBILISATION ON 31ST JULY, AND FRANCE AND GERMANY FOLLOWED SUIT THE NEXT DAY. GERMANY DECLARED WAR ON FRANCE ON 3RD AUGUST.

THE SUNDAY NEWS WAR MAP, 1914

RESPONSES TO WAR

The First World War, and the policies introduced because of it, sometimes met resistance, protest and unrest away from the front lines.

WOMEN'S INTERNATIONAL CONGRESS

In 1915, women from many countries who were seeking the vote also wanted to end the war. They decided to organise a Women's International Congress in neutral Netherlands. **The conference was held in The Hague, and was attended by approximately 2,000 women from 26 countries.**

The French and Russian governments banned attendance, and the British tried to prevent women from going. 180 British women applied for travel permits, but only 24 were issued. The Admiralty then closed the North Sea to all shipping on their day of departure. **All except two British women were prevented from going**, and the press mocked them as 'Peace Crankettes'!

Although secret peace feelers began from autumn 1914, the Congress was the first international meeting to outline plans for a peace settlement. The 20 resolutions, which included no secret treaties, are reflected in the Covenant of the League of Nations (see page 126) that was signed after the war. The Congress also agreed that no blame should be assigned for starting the war.

City of London Police.

NOTICE TO ALIEN ENEMIES.

BETWEEN THE HOURS OF 9 P.M. & 5 A.M.

male alien enemies are required, with effect from 18th May, to remain at their registered places of residence unless furnished with a permit from the Registration Officer of the Registration District in which that place of residence is situate.

The Police are directed to enforce this restriction.

CITY POLICE OFFICE,
26, OLD JEWRY,
LONDON, E.C.
11th May, 1915.

J. W. NOTT-BOWER,
Commissioner of Police in the City of London

Defence of the Realm Act poster.

ENEMY ALIENS

Prior to the outbreak of War, there were over 50,000 Germans living in Britain, most of whom were resident in London but also in places such as Brighton and Birmingham. The British Government introduced the Aliens Restriction Act in 1914 immediately after the outbreak of the War which meant **Germans had to register with the police and could not leave Britain without a special permit**.

The Government also introduced a policy of interning German males of military age. This was said to be for their safety, but was mainly to stop them being able to enlist into the German army. Internment camps emerged across the country; the largest could hold up to 23,000 and was situated on the Isle of Man (see page 45).

DON'T WAIT FOR CONSCRIPTION - GO AND HELP!

Patriotic slogan.

DID YOU KNOW...?

GEORGE KENNER WAS A GERMAN ARTIST WHO MOVED TO LONDON IN 1910. DURING THE WAR GEORGE WAS HELD AT THREE INTERNMENT CAMPS, WHICH INSPIRED A LOT OF HIS ARTWORK.

Conscription was introduced in New Zealand in 1916 and Canada in 1917.

CONSCRIPTION IN BRITAIN

The First World War was fought by mass armies, mostly raised by conscription. However, in 1914 Britain's military relied on volunteers, and its initial expansion was achieved without resort to compulsion. By 1916 the supply of volunteers could no longer match demand, especially as losses mounted, and Britain also needed to achieve a more rational division of labour between essential war work and military service. So the British Government introduced conscription through the Military Service Act 1916. **Single men aged 18 to 41 were liable to be called up for military service under the Act.** Conscription was generally accepted as necessary, but men were able to appeal to a local tribunal for exemption from Military Service (see page 102).

One hour before dinner – waiting to get hot water for dishwashing: painting by George Kenner, a German artist interned in Britain during the war.

OBJECTIONS TO WAR IN GERMANY

Military values were an important part of German society, but there were people who objected to the War. **Anti-war feelings were suppressed by military censorship, and pacifists were isolated and imprisoned.**

Conscription laws in Germany (see page 32) did not allow people to object to the war, but men who objected for religious reasons were often given non-combatant roles. However, those who objected for political reasons were often sent to mental asylums or prisons! This was a way of discrediting those who refused to take up non-combatant roles, and getting rid of troublesome individuals.

CONSCRIPTION ELSEWHERE

France: Conscription had a huge impact on French society, with up to 80% of men aged between 18 and 46 serving in the war by 1915. The French government turned to their colonies and, like Britain, to Chinese labourers for additional manpower.

Russia: Prior to the war, men were conscripted into the army for three years. In 1914, it is claimed that Russia had an army of over five million men. Its problem was the production of the weapons needed to equip them.

Austria-Hungary: Three armed forces were obtained by conscription. Austria and Hungary each had its own territorial army, while the regular Imperial and Royal Army conscripted from across the Empire.

The Ottoman Empire: Conscription was enforced, regardless of religion. The empire faced many challenges in mobilising troops for the war, not least the effect on a peasant economy of taking men from the land. Fighting on multiple fronts without completed railway networks stretched its resources.

DID YOU KNOW...?

IN 1917 THE BRITISH ROYAL FAMILY CHANGED THEIR NAME FROM THE GERMAN-SOUNDING SAXE-COBURG AND GOTHA TO WINDSOR.

MAJOR BATTLES

BATTLE OF MONS

The Battle of Mons was the **first British battle of the First World War** and the last of four 'Battles of the Frontiers' on the Western Front between Allied and German forces.

On 22nd August 1914 the British Expeditionary Force (BEF), led by British Commander-in-Chief Field Marshal **Sir John French**, dug defensive positions near the Mons Canal as a result of British intelligence warning that the size and vicinity of the German army was not known.

Von Kluck, commander of the German First army, engaged the British in battle on 23rd August and although the BEF were heavily outnumbered, they withstood six hours of constant shelling and infantry assault.

By evening, French ordered his army to retreat after realising the size of the German army.

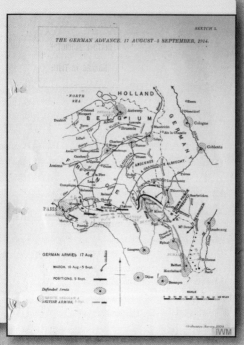

Map of the German lines at Mons.

BATTLE OF THE SOMME

The Battle of the Somme started on 1st July 1916 and lasted until November of the same year. The British planned to attack German trenches along a 15-mile front north of the River Somme with French divisions attacking along an 8-mile front south of the river. **The battle started with a week-long artillery bombardment** of German lines – a total of 1.6 million shells were fired – in an attempt to destroy the German trenches. However, all did not go to plan. Many of the British shells failed to explode, and when the bombardment began German troops moved to the deep dugouts in their trenches which offered relative safety from attack. Germans waited for the shelling to end and set up machine guns ready for their counter-attack. The British suffered 60,000 casualties, of whom 20,000 died on the first day, marking it as one of the biggest defeats the British army had ever suffered. Over the course of the next few months, the British suffered around 420,000 casualties.

British soldiers eating hot rations in the Ancre Valley during the Battle of the Somme, October 1916.

DID YOU KNOW...?

TRENCHES WERE DUG IN ZIGZAG LINES, SO THE BLAST OF AN ARTILLERY SHELL LANDING IN THEM COULD AFFECT ONLY A SHORT LENGTH OF THE TRENCH.

FIRST BATTLE OF THE MARNE

Sir John French and the BEF retreated from Mons alongside the French Army as far as the River Marne, just outside Paris. On 6th September 1914, **French Commander-in-Chief Joseph Joffre** ordered an attack on the advancing German forces.

The offensive managed to increase the gap between the German First and Second Armies which was exploited by the BEF and French Army, who advanced in a counter-attack against the Germans.

The attack succeeded, and German forces were in full retreat by 11th September. When they reached an area near the River Aisne they dug defensive trenches to repel the attack from the Allied forces, **marking the beginning of the trench warfare that dominated much of the First World War.**

Village of Pozières, France by Richard C. Carline. A battle-scarred landscape with a road running horizontally across the composition in the foreground. There are two trucks, one marked with a red cross, and four soldiers on horseback moving along the road.

A drawing of Welsh soldiers by Muirhead Bone.

BATTLE OF CAMBRAI

The Battle of Cambrai is noted as the **first battle to use tanks en masse** combined with heavy artillery, infantry, cavalry and air power. The Allies started their coordinated attack on 20th November 1917 and proved successful at surprising the Germans. Bombs were dropped on German anti-tank guns to clear the path for the Allied tanks and ground troops, and artillery was used to cover the troops from a German counter-attack.

The initial attack gained considerable distance, but the success of the attack did not last long: for example, a strategic bridge collapsed under the weight of a tank, which halted the advance of cavalry into Cambrai. There was a breakdown in command which opened the Allies up to the German counter-attack resulting in the Germans recovering much of the land that was lost. There were **44,000 British casualties** by the time the battle ended on 6th December.

Fighting on the front lines is fierce, but to keep up morale my men and I spend most of our time in the support trenches... things are much quieter there.

MAJOR BATTLES

BATTLE OF JUTLAND

The German commander, **Admiral Reinhardt von Scheer**, hoped to lure out **Admiral Beatty's** Battlecruiser and **Admiral Jellicoe's** Grand Fleet from major British naval bases to waiting submarines and surface boats. Scheer hoped to destroy Beatty before Jellicoe arrived; however, the British were warned by their codebreakers, and Jellicoe ordered the Grand Fleet to put to sea early.

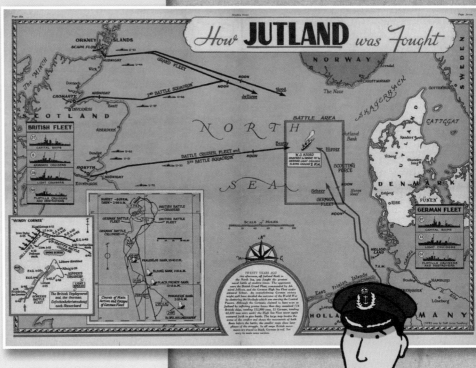

The Battle of Jutland started on 31st May 1916 when Beatty encountered Admiral Hipper's German battlecruisers starting an artillery duel at 15,000 yards. The Germans were successful in damaging HMS *Lion* and sank HMS *Indefatigable* and HMS *Queen Mary*. After this initial encounter, Beatty turned north and lured the Germans onto Jellicoe's Grand Fleet.

The Germans thought Jellicoe's fleet were too far north to intervene and so received a nasty surprise when they found themselves under bombardment from the Grand Fleet. Scheer ordered a retreat and after a night of intense fighting the German battleships successfully made it to harbour.

The Battle of Jutland was the only major encounter between the British and German fleets in the First World War. Admiral Jellicoe had 24 dreadnoughts ready for sea just a few hours after his return to Scapa Flow. Admiral Scheer had only 10, and repairs to his ships took considerably longer to complete, leaving the German Fleet effectively blockaded into port after Jutland.

Land ahoy! My name is Captain Chris and I fought at the Battle of Jutland with my fellow sailors.

THE THIRD BATTLE OF YPRES

The Third Battle of Ypres, better known to many as Passchendaele due to the heavy fighting and loss of life near that village, was launched by the Allies in Belgium on 31st July 1917. The aim of the campaign was the destruction of German submarine bases on the Belgian coast, thus requiring clearance of the bases on the Belgian coast. British forces and Australian and New Zealand **(ANZAC)** forces launched a heavy artillery attack on the Germans; however, the main targets of the Allied offensive remained out of reach due to the poor conditions of thick mud caused by heavy rainfall in early August.

By October the Allied attackers were nearing exhaustion as German forces were reinforced by reserves released from the Eastern Front. The Germans used mustard gas to aid their defence which resulted in chemical burns.

The **Canadians were sent to relieve the ANZAC forces** early in October and take part in the push to capture Passchendaele. The eventual capture of Passchendaele village by British and Canadian forces came on 6th November and finally allowed British General Haig to cut off the offensive. (Haig had taken over from Sir John French as Commander-in-Chief of the BEF in December 1915). Although the Battle of Passchendaele was claimed as a victory, it came at the cost of **245,000 British casualties as opposed to 215,000 on the German side**.

Gassed. 'In Arduis Fidelis' by war artist Gilbert Rogers (1881–1956). The body of a dead soldier lies on his back on a battlefield. The body rests rigidly on a thick mound of mud: the feet hang into a small rain-filled crater.

At the battle of Jutland, the Royal Navy suffered over 6,000 casualties and the German fleet suffered over 3,000.

DID YOU KNOW...?

BATTLE OF PASSCHENDAELE: THE AREA IN FLANDERS WAS SATURATED WITH THE HEAVIEST RAINFALL FOR 30 YEARS, AND CONSTANT ARTILLERY BOMBARDMENT BY THE ALLIES CHURNED THE CLAY SOIL AND SMASHED THE DRAINAGE SYSTEMS. SHELL CRATERS FILLED WITH WATER PRODUCED THICK MUD THAT CLOGGED UP RIFLES AND IMMOBILISED TANKS. THE SWAMP-LIKE CONDITIONS BECAME SO DEEP IN MANY PLACES THAT MEN AND HORSES DROWNED IN IT.

A NEW KIND OF WARFARE

The First World War initiated major transformations which led to recognisably modern forms of warfare. The arms race between the two warring sides hastened the development of more efficient and destructive weapons.

GUNS

The most common rifle issued to British troops was the Short Magazine Lee Enfield (SMLE) rifle (see diagram), which was manually operated and contained 10 rounds in two five-round clips. The SMLE was **capable of rapid fire in the hands of a highly trained professional**.

Machine guns were also introduced as infantry weapons, and their reliability made them effective at inflicting high numbers of casualties. The German 'Maxim' machine gun was able to fire as many as 600 rounds a minute, and was used to deadly effect during the Battle of the Somme (see page 12). German troops tactically placed their machine guns on the front line, and **within minutes of the battle starting thousands of British troops were killed**.

The Gas Mask by Irish artist William Orpen (1878–1931). A study of a stretcher-bearer sitting beside a stretcher, his face obscured by the gas mask he is wearing.

GAS

During the First World War many different gases were experimented with and used as weapons, resulting in horrific injuries, although many proved transient and gas was not as lethal as first presumed.

Chlorine was first used on the Western Front on 22nd April 1915 during the Second Battle of Ypres. It was used on the Eastern Front earlier, but the cold seems to have limited its effect. It is a yellowy-green gas with a distinctive smell. It caused coughing, vomiting and eye irritation. And if there was enough of it, it could even cause death! Early in the war it caused a lot of casualties but these lessened when the gas mask was invented.

Phosgene was first used 19th December 1915. It was harder to detect, as it is colourless with a faint smell. Phosgene was the most deadly of the three, causing 85% of all gas-related deaths during the war. When exposed to the gas victims experienced breathing problems and the full impact of suffocation could be delayed for up to 48 hours!

Mustard gas was first used on 12th July 1917. It became a frequently used chemical weapon, causing many injuries, especially to the victims' sight (see page 115). It is a yellowy-brown gas that could and did cause fatal chemical burns, as well as impacting on a person's eyes and breathing. Although it did not kill a huge number of people, it caused a lot of suffering and troops were particularly afraid of it.

A SOLDIER'S EQUIPMENT

Brodie Helmet

This was the first metal helmet worn by British troops. It was only issued in the latter years of the war – at first soldiers fought in cloth caps.

Belt items

On his belt the soldier has a water bottle, entrenching tool, sheath for his bayonet, extra ammunition pouches, and a small haversack for food and other supplies.

Puttees

These were strips of cloth wrapped tightly around the lower leg for support and protection. The word comes from the Hindi word *patti*, meaning bandage.

1908 Pattern Webbing

The soldier is wearing battle dress containing all the essential supplies for fighting, minus the large rucksack worn while on the march. The small front pouches are for ammunition.

Rank badge

This man is a sergeant, meaning he was in charge of a troop or platoon of around 30 soldiers.

Short Magazine Lee-Enfield MkIII

Chambering a .303 round, the SMLE was designed as a reliable, accurate rifle, and was used throughout the War by troops fighting for the British Empire.

DID YOU KNOW...?

THIS WAR WAS THE FIRST CONFLICT TO WITNESS POISON GAS BEING USED EFFECTIVELY – SOME SOLDIERS DIED A LINGERING DEATH AS THEIR LUNGS COLLAPSED AND FILLED WITH LIQUID; OTHERS WERE BLINDED FOR LIFE.

TO PROTECT THEMSELVES FROM POTENTIAL ATTACKS, SOLDIERS WOULD WEAR PROTECTIVE HELMETS, WHICH CONSISTED OF FACE MASKS, GOGGLES AND RESPIRATORS.

A NEW KIND OF WARFARE

ARTILLERY

Large guns used on land are known as artillery. Artillery supported lighter or so-called field guns by firing high-explosive shells to destroy trenches and field fortifications.

Before the First World War, 'ranging shots' would be used to establish an enemy's position. However, this made a surprise attack impossible, so **once war broke out scientists began searching for ways to target enemy positions accurately without firing ranging shots first.**

A Gun Hospital, by Scottish artist Sir Muirhead Bone (1876–1953).

The principal use for aircraft in 1914-15 was for reconnaissance and aerial photography. Pilots and their observers could spot enemy artillery batteries and direct fire (see page 74).

A new technique to improve the impact of artillery was sound ranging, where microphones were used to detect the sound waves of a gun being fired. By measuring the time between the sound waves it was possible to determine the position of an enemy's gun.

Time fuses were developed and designed to make shells explode while still in the air, to shower and injure ground soldiers with shrapnel. However, these fuses burned unpredictably, and everyone involved in the conflict raced to find the solution first. The Germans created a clockwork fuse that was not affected by the atmosphere or altitude, making their artillery much more effective. By 1917 the British had adopted a fuse which exploded on impact, so that its force spread sideways before it could bury itself in the ground.

TANKS

In January 1915 the idea of the tank or 'Land Battleship' was beginning to be seen as a necessary war weapon to withstand machine-gun fire, act as a shield for advancing troops and break through trench defences. **Tanks were used for the first time at the Battle of the Somme in September 1916.** The early models were not very successful; after short journeys in the tanks, men would no longer be fit to work because the conditions inside were so awful! Although the tanks caught the enemy by surprise, their flaws quickly became apparent and often caused more damage to the occupants than the Germans! Later models played a vital role in the Allied advances of 1918.

Tanks by William Orpen. A view looking up to the underside of two tanks. The tanks are cresting a low rise, their treads rearing up towards the grey sky..

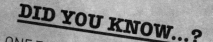

DID YOU KNOW...?

ONE TACTIC USED TO HEAR THE GERMANS WAS FILLING A BISCUIT TIN WITH WATER. THIS WAY, WHEN THE GERMAN TUNNELLERS APPROACHED, THE VIBRATIONS WOULD CAUSE A RIPPLE IN THE WATER!

TUNNELLING

Lieutenant-Colonel Sir John Norton-Griffths MP recruited civilian miners with little military training for the Royal Engineers' tunnelling companies. Their task was to go 100 feet underground and tunnel their way to the other side. He knew these miners had been working underground since childhood, and he believed it was that experience that would make them better, faster and quieter tunnellers than the Germans.

Tunnelling was a dangerous job. The fear of carbon monoxide poisoning or the tunnel collapsing was always present, but **the main worry was that the tunnellers would meet the enemy underground in fierce hand-to-hand fighting** or be detected and buried alive. The key to tunnelling was being very quiet and being able to locate the opposition before they found you. From November 1915 tunnellers were able to use a Geophone, a device that picked up sounds from up to 100 feet away, allowing them to track the enemy, find the position that would cause most damage, and blow them up.

Tunnelling became a vital part of the war. By May 1916 there were three Canadian, one New Zealand and three Australian Tunnelling Companies working on the Western Front. The key to success underground was hearing and killing the enemy before they heard and killed you.

This official photograph shows German soldiers in trenches on the Western Front.

My name is Molly, and my fellow workers and I produce shells for the artillery.

WOMEN AT THE FRONT

WOMEN'S ARMY AUXILIARY CORPS (WAAC)

After the heavy losses of men on the Somme in the summer of 1916, it was decided that women should be used in the army. Lieutenant General Henry Lawson estimated that 12,000 soldiers working in non-combatant roles on the Lines of Communications in France could be freed for front line service by women taking on their jobs.

The Corps did not have the same status as men; instead of ranks it had grades – officers were called 'Officials' and Non-Commissioned Officers were called 'Forewomen' and other ranks were called 'Workers'. Like the women working in munitions factories and other civilian jobs, they were paid less than their male counterparts. The WAAC were employed in a variety of jobs, including cooking and waiting on officers, and serving as clerks, telephone operators, store-women, drivers, printers, bakers and cemetery gardeners.

Queen Mary became the patron of the Corps, and thus it was renamed Queen Mary's Army Auxiliary Corps (QMAAC) on 9th April 1918. **By 1918, nearly 40,000 women had enrolled** in the QMAAC. Of these, some 7,000 served on the Western Front, the rest back in the United Kingdom. With the end of the war, the QMAAC were no longer of use in an army being cut down in size to peacetime levels, and so the QMAAC was formally disbanded on 27th September 1921.

Recruitment poster for the WAAC.

A half-length portrait of a young female Russian serving with the Russian Women's 'Battalion of Death' in 1917.

DID YOU KNOW...?

IN 1917, RUSSIA WITNESSED THOUSANDS OF MEN DESERTING THE RANKS. IN RESPONSE, MARIA BOCHKAREVA PERSUADED THE RUSSIAN GOVERNMENT TO SET UP A WOMEN'S UNIT. THE WOMEN'S BATTALION, THE SO-CALLED 'BATTALION OF DEATH', WAS 2,000 STRONG IN THE BEGINNING BUT DECREASED TO JUST 250.

BETTY STEVENSON (1896-1918)

Bertha 'Betty' Stevenson was born in York on 3rd September 1896. Betty's parents were activists in the YMCA, and she became heavily involved at a very young age.

In January 1916, one of Betty's aunts went to France to manage a YMCA Canteen in St Denis Hut on the outskirts of Paris. Betty was keen to join her. At 19, she was considered too young, but a month later she went anyway, paying her own expenses. She enjoyed the work, writing:

'We know how grateful the men are, and they know us now so well, I somehow feel it would be mean to leave them for a new place.'

Once her term at St Denis was completed, Betty returned to the UK, but she was soon anxious to get back to France. **In April 1917 she was posted to Étaples as a YMCA driver**, responsible for transporting lecturers, concert parties and relatives from England visiting the wounded in hospital.

Betty was killed by an air raid the following year having, despite the danger, stayed in the area to assist some French refugees.

She was given a military funeral and was posthumously awarded the Croix de Guerre avec Palme by General Pétain for courage and devotion to duty.

The personal inscription on her headstone reads simply, 'The Happy Warrior'.

Betty described Étaples in a letter to her father:

'I'm awfully fond of the river here. There is a bridge over it from which you can get the most wonderful view of everything. On one side the river mouth and the sea and the little fishing boats; the quay and the big sailor's crucifix, where the women pray when there is a storm at sea. The boats anchor quite near; and they look like something hazy and unreal, sitting on a shiny wet river; with every sail and mast and man reflected in the water. Behind them are houses – filthy and ramshackle, but with the sun warming their pink, white and grey roofs. Behind the houses again is the camp – the tents crawling up the hill like white snails, and more hills and pines behind them. The whole thing is so illogical, boats and fisherman on the one hand, and on the other, war.'

DID YOU KNOW...?

FLORA SANDES WAS THE ONLY BRITISH WOMAN TO SERVE OFFICIALLY AS A SOLDIER IN THE FIRST WORLD WAR. AT THE OUTBREAK OF WAR SHE JOINED AN AMBULANCE UNIT IN SERBIA. THE SERBIAN ARMY SUFFERED HEAVY LOSSES IN 1915 AND RETREATED INTO ALBANIA, AT WHICH TIME FLORA OFFICIALLY ENROLLED AS A SOLDIER WITH A SERBIAN REGIMENT.

POETRY

The poetry of the First World War has become so popular that the phrase 'war poetry' is now taken to mean not war poetry in general (there have been poems written about every war), but only the poetry of the First World War.

War poetry is as complex as the war itself and the people who fought in it. Many of the best-known poets were killed in the war, and never saw their poems published. Some lived on, but a number never seemed to scale the poetic heights they had reached in the war.

Some poets, such as Rupert Brooke, took pride in the war, whilst others, such as Siegfried Sassoon (see page 107) and Wilfred Owen, wrote bitterly against what they saw as its pointless sacrifice. In between these two extremes, the war poets expressed every possible opinion. The best-known poems and poets are those who were clearly outraged by the scenes on the front lines of the battlefields.

The Soldier – *Rupert Brooke (1887–1915)*

If I should die think only this of me
That there's some corner of a foreign field
That is forever England. There shall be
In that rich earth a richer dust concealed;
A dust whom England bore, shaped, made aware,
Gave once, her flowers to love, her ways to roam,
A body of England's, breathing English air,
Washed by the rivers, blest by the suns of home.
And think, this heart, all evil shed away,
A pulse in the eternal mind, no less
Gives somewhere back the thoughts by England given;
Her sights and sounds; dreams happy as her day;
And laughter, learnt of friends; and gentleness,
In hearts at peace, under an English heaven.

Do you think everyone supported the war in the same way that Rupert Brooke did?

Fighting Hard
Henry Lawson (1867–1922)

Rolling out to fight for England,
  singing songs across the sea;

Rolling north to fight for England,
  and to fight for you and me.

Fighting hard for France and England,
where the storms of death are hurled;

Fighting hard for Australasia
and the honour of the World!

Fighting hard.

Fighting hard for little Tassy,
where the apple orchards grow;

(And the northern territory,
just to give the place a show),

Fighting hard for Home and Empire,
while the Commonwealth prevails—

And, in spite of all her blunders,
dying hard for New South Wales.

Dying hard.

Home Thoughts – *Unknown, 1916*

The hot, red rocks of Aden
  Stand from their burnished sea;
  The bitter sands of Aden
  Lie shimmering in their lee.

We have no joy of battle,
  No honour here is won;
  Our little fights are nameless,
  With Turk and sand and sun

East and west the greater wars
  Swirl wildly up and down;
  Forgotten here and sadly
  We hold the Port and Town.

The great round trees of England
  Swell nobly from the grass,
  The dark green fields of England,
  Through which the red cows pass.

The wild-flowered lanes of England
  Hurt us with vain desire;
  The little wayside cottage,
  The clanging blacksmith's fire.

The salt, dry sands of Aden,
  The bitter, sun-cursed shore;
  Forget us not in England,
  We cannot serve you more.

Dead Man's Dump – *Isaac Rosenberg (1890–1918)*

They lie there huddled, friend and foeman,
Man born of man, and born of woman;
And shells go crying over them,
From night till night and now …

Burnt black by strange decay
Their sinister faces lie,
The lid over each eye;
The grass and coloured clay
More motion have than they…

ANIMALS

Despite the advancement in weaponry during the First World War, animals were heavily relied upon by all sides, both physically and psychologically. They took on a multitude of roles, such as transport and communications. Horses and dogs were considered so essential on the battlefield that gas masks were made for them.

A British war dog wears a gas mask as it is held by its handler at the army kennels near Étaples. Rows of kennels are clearly visible in the background.

DOGS

Dogs were some of the most trusted workers during the war and took on a variety of roles depending on their size, intelligence and training. Sadly, thousands of dogs were lost to disease, starvation, exhaustion and enemy attack.

Sentry dogs: These were typically Dobermanns and would stay with one owner to act as a guard dog. They were trained to give a warning signal such as a growl or snarl to indicate when there was an unknown presence in the area.

Scout dogs: These were highly trained in avoiding detection. They would accompany soldiers on foot patrol and could detect enemy scent up to 1,000 yards away. To avoid drawing attention to the squad, a scout dog would stiffen, raise its hackles and point its tail.

Messenger dogs: These dogs helped to get messages to the front line and from one base to another. Dogs were able to travel over any terrain a lot faster than humans and presented less of a target to a sniper.

A MAN'S BEST FRIEND

Lieutenant-Colonel Edwin Hautenville Richardson began training dogs for military purposes in 1900 after learning of a German purchasing large quantities of collie dogs for the German Army on behalf of his government. Richardson bought land for farming at Carnoustie on the east coast of Scotland with his wife Blanche Bannon where they pursued their mutual interest in canine training. Officers at the nearby Barry Buddon army camp took an interest in their work and allowed Richardson to bring his dogs in to experiment during the training of soldiers. **Richardson and Blanche were eventually asked by The War Office to set up the first British War Dog School at Shoeburyness, Essex.**

My name is Scruffs and I was a casualty dog in the war. My handler from the Royal Army Medical Corps sent me to soldiers with medical supplies so they could tend to their own wounds until medics could reach them or they could make it back to British lines.

DID YOU KNOW...?

THE IMPERIAL CAMEL CORPS BRIGADE WAS A CAMEL-MOUNTED INFANTRY BRIGADE THAT SERVED IN THE MIDDLE EAST FOR THE ALLIES. THE UNIT INCLUDED ONE BATTALION EACH FROM GREAT BRITAIN AND NEW ZEALAND, AND TWO FROM AUSTRALIA.

The Long Patrol: The Wadi by James McBey (1883–1959). An Imperial Camel Corps patrol halts in a wadi (dried-out riverbed) in the desert.

PIGEONS

Approximately **100,000 pigeons were used as messengers during the war**. They always flew home when released, so the troops had to ensure that there were nests placed where they needed messages sent to. Pigeons were strapped into corsets and dropped by parachute at designated 'drop zones' for secret agents working behind enemy lines.

Coo! My name is Polly and I was a messenger pigeon during the war. I was much more reliable at delivering messages than man-made machinery! I even carried coded messages to and from secret agents working behind enemy lines!

There were thousands of us living in the trenches along the Western Front. We made the trenches very dirty, spread diseases and fed on delicious rotting food! We also fed on decomposing bodies.

I had up to 800-900 babies every year so trenches would be literally infested with my family and friends!

ANIMALS

At the start of the war, horses were used mostly by the cavalry – soldiers who fought on horseback using swords and guns. However, due to the nature of trench warfare on the Western Front and the development of machine guns, cavalry charges could no longer be used, so horses were used for transportation instead.

HORSES

As the war was initially presumed to be 'over by Christmas', the Army Medical Services did not initially invest in motorised ambulances, but used horse power to take the wounded to first aid stations. The horses suffered almost as much as the casualties during the long and difficult journeys over shell-cratered terrain.

In 1914 the British Army owned 25,000 horses but this was not considered enough, so thousands more were requisitioned from rural Britain and purchased from countries around the world, such as the United States, Canada, New Zealand, South Africa, India, Spain, Portugal and Argentina. **While the Allies were able to import horses, the Central Powers could only replace their losses by conquest, and requisitioned many from Belgium, France and Ukraine**.

It is estimated that around **eight million horses from all sides died during the war**.

A Horse Ambulance Pulling a Sick Horse out of a Field, by Edwin Noble (1876–1941). Two strong horses draw a deep cart over the brow of a hill. Their hooves send up clouds of dust that cover the soldier who walks alongside. The bony frame of an ill horse can be seen standing in the cart.

My name is Duke and I was a war horse. I carried food and weapons to the front lines and pulled field guns into position. It was thirsty work!

We tried our hardest to boost the morale of the soldiers.

BLUE CROSS FUND FOR HORSES

Although mechanised ambulances eventually replaced horses, horses continued to be used for all other work. Lady Smith-Dorrien, wife of General Sir Horace Smith-Dorrien, became President of the Blue Cross Fund for Horses which provided veterinary surgeons and hospitals for wounded horses. **One fund-raising initiative was the publication of a *Book of Poems for the Blue Cross Fund*.** Several poems are by children; the youngest contributor was Inez Quilter, aged 11. She lived in Suffolk and would have seen the Army requisitioning the carthorses that had previously been used for farm work.

An Answer to Cavalry Charger
Helena Robinson

We've read your appeal, faithful charger
There is truth in the story you tell,
So we're sending you on a subscription.
And hope others will do so as well.
You deserve all our help and pity.
For you have helped our soldiers so true,
To fight for their dear Country's honour,
And you have shared in their sorrows, too.

You've borne the brunt of battle bravely.
Now you are badly wounded and torn.
You want our kind care and attention.
And need rest for your body so worn.
You shall have it, true-hearted charger.
We will tell of your right noble fall.
Then others will help to restore you,
And respond to your sad-hearted call.

You are but a cavalry charger,
Yet the God that made us, made you,
So we'll pray for you and your comrades. And we
know God will answer us, too.
We'll uphold the work of the ''Blue Cross.''
We will do just as much as we can.
To help you, dear cavalry charger.
For we know you're the true friend of man.

Sall – *Inez Quilter*

I'm none of yer London gentry,
Non o' yer Hyde Park swells,
But I'm only a farmers plough horse
And I'se born among hills and fells.
Yer mus'n't expect no graces
Fer yer won't get 'em from me,
I'se made as nature intended
An' I'm jus' plain Sall, d'ye see.

You've not seen me in the Row yet
An; yer won't, if yer try so 'ard,
I'm not a show 'orse yer forget
But I'm Sall, plain Sall, and Sall goes 'ard!

DID YOU KNOW...?

ELEPHANTS FILLED IN FOR ABSENT HORSES IN RURAL AND INDUSTRIAL BRITAIN, AND PULLED HEAVY GUNS ON THE FRONT LINES.

FIGHTING ON MULTIPLE FRONTS

The Western Front is the best-known battlefield of the First World War, but fighting took place across the globe.

LIFE IN THE TRENCHES

The Western Front was plagued by trench warfare and conditions were much worse at the beginning of the war. The Allied trenches of 1914 were just deep furrows which provided minimal cover from enemy fire. This was because the generals believed that trench warfare was only temporary as the 'normal' war of movement would resume in the spring.

A condition known as **Trench Foot** caused by the cold, wet and unsanitary conditions could cause fungal infections and feet were amputated in severe cases. Trenches were often smelly and unsanitary; this was because dead bodies were buried nearby, and there was a huge infestation of rats and lice spreading disease and infection.

The British front line west of Trescault before the Battle of Cambrai on 10th December 1917.

CAPTURE OF SAMOA

Samoa, an island in the Pacific Ocean close to New Zealand, was a German colony in 1914. A German wireless station was established on the island, and Australian intelligence found out that it was protected by 80 men and a gunboat. **Colonel Robert Logan led 1,400 New Zealand troops with an escort of three 'P' Class cruisers from the Royal Navy's New Zealand Station to capture Samoa**. Samoa was under Allied control by 29th August 1914. After Togoland in West Africa, this was the second territory the Allies gained in the War.

New Zealand soldiers landing on Samoa in the Southern winter of 1914 at the start of their occupation of the Pacific island.

THE SIEGE OF TSINGTAO

Germany built a port and naval base at Tsingtao, a city in eastern Shandong Province on the east coast of China. The base was stationed by approximately 4,000 troops. Japan was allied with Britain from 1902 and declared war on Germany on 23rd August 1914. **Japan led the Allied capture of Tsingtao with a couple of the Royal Navy's China Squadron ships in support**. This campaign violated Chinese neutrality and was the only battle to be fought in the Far East during the First World War.

On 12th August 1914 Gold Coast-born Sergeant-Major Alhaji Grunshi fired the first shot in the war.

CHINESE LABOUR CORPS

China proclaimed neutrality from the outset of war; however, the ruling powers decreed China had to get involved in the war in 1916. **China sent 140,000 labourers to assist the British and French** on the front lines in Europe, 100,000 of whom served in Flanders, Belgium. Chinese volunteers were paid up to four times more than labourers back in China, and their work included digging trenches, working in factories and carrying ammunition.

China later declared war on Germany and Austria-Hungary in 1917, and the Chinese Labour Corps served under British officers. The war claimed many Chinese lives, and many of the victims are buried in cemeteries dotted across the Flemish landscape.

Chinese Working in a Quarry by British Surrealist and war artist Paul Nash (1889–1946).

My name is Sepoy Joti. I fought with the Indian army in Gallipoli and Mesopotamia, as well as on the Western Front.

DID YOU KNOW...?

TRENCHES WERE NEVER TRULY DEVELOPED ALONG THE EASTERN FRONT (RUSSIA) AS FIGHTING WAS STRETCHED ALONG A LONGER FRONT LINE. THIS ENABLED MORE MOBILITY THAN WAS EXPERIENCED ON THE WESTERN FRONT.

I loved it in the trenches!

THE SALONIKA CAMPAIGN

On 5th October 1915 the first British and French troops landed at the Greek port in Salonika (now called Thessaloniki). During the almost three-year campaign, the British Salonika Force (BSF), French, Greek, Italian, Russian and Serbian contingents fought together at various points.

THE CAMPAIGN

The BSF aimed to stop Bulgarian forces from joining the German and Austro-Hungarian attack on Serbia. **With early Allied failures and German successes, Bulgaria saw a real possibility that the Central Powers would win the war**, and so they joined them and declared war on Serbia on 13th October 1915.

By 14th December the Allies were forced to retreat into Greek territory towards Salonika. Although the Allies had 250,000 men, they lacked the necessary equipment and supplies to fight along a 250-mile front. The front stretched from Albania to the mouth of the River Struma in Greece.

Many operations were launched throughout the three years, but the Allied failure to break Bulgarian resistance resulted in a stalemate along

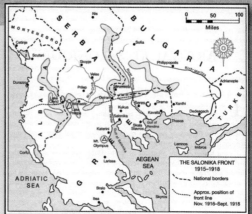

A contemporary map showing the Salonika Front.

the Salonika Front. It was not until 1918 that a surprise French and Serbian attack managed to break through the Bulgarian lines. The Salonika Campaign was long and dangerous, ending with the surrender of Bulgaria on 26th September 1918 (see page 123).

THE BATTLE OF KOSTURINO

On 20th November 1915, Irish troops took over a front-line ridge that ran between Kosturino, now a village in the Former Yugoslav Republic of Macedonia, and the Greek border at Lake Doiran. Their aim was to stop Bulgarian forces advancing and cutting off escape lines, as well as hiding the Allied forces' retreat to Salonika.

At Kosturino, the ground was hard and rocky, so the trenches were just two feet deep, offering little protection from Bulgarian artillery and machine-gun fire. Protecting a small mount, which the British called Rocky Peak, was essential for holding the ridge.

On 7th December the Bulgarians attacked and seized Rocky Peak, before turning their attention

to the trenches filled with Irish servicemen. A new front line was established, the Bulgarians did not follow up with an attack, so the Irish were able to hold their new position for a couple of days. The French troops were able to retreat with the Irish following to the Greek side of the border, where the Bulgarians were ordered to stop. By the 20th December, British and French troops had returned to Salonika.

When the French and British got to Salonika they surrounded themselves in barbed wire for protection. The area became known as The Birdcage!

OWEN RUTTER (1889-1944)

Major Owen Rutter spent a lot of his war career in the Salonika Campaign, fighting in the Battle of Horseshoe Hill (August 1916) and the Battles of Doiran. However, he is best known for his poem, **The Song of Tiadatha** (a pun on 'Tired Arthur'). It was a parody of Longfellow's *The Song of Hiawatha*.

The poem was published in sections under Owen's fake name Klip-Klip in *Balkan News*, a troop newspaper that ran from 1915 to 1919. The main character, Tired Arthur, is a very human and recognisable figure. The poem tells the story of a man volunteering to fight in the war, seeing action, being injured and returning home on leave. The poem was very popular with the troops and was printed as a book in Salonika in 1919.

The Song of Tiadatha – *Owen Rutter*

Who on earth was Tiadatha?
A youth of two and twenty summers.
You could see him any morning
In July of 1914,
Strolling slowly down St James's
From his comfy flat in Duke Street.
Little cared he of in those days,
Save of socks and ties and hair wash,
Girls and motor-cars and suppers.
There were many Tired Arthurs
In July of 1914.
Then came war, and Tiadatha
Read his papers every morning,
Read the posters on the hoardings,
Read "Your King and Country want you."

[extract]

The BSF suffered over 160,000 cases of malaria, assistance from voluntary medical organisations, such as the Scottish Women's Hospitals (see page 43), proved invaluable.

SPORTS FIELD DAY

Throughout the First World War, sports played an important part in boosting morale and entertaining those serving (see page 72). **In May 1916, Allied troops stationed near Salonika organised a Sports Field Day** and many officers, soldiers and medical staff joined in.

The Macedonian Campaign: a gymnastic display by men of an Indian transport unit at a sports meeting near Salonika in May 1916.

GERMANY

Kaiser Wilhelm II, King of Prussia and Emperor of Germany, was determined to expand Germany's power and when the First World War broke out most Germans were in support. However, as the war continued discontent increased on the German Home Front.

CONSCRIPTION IN GERMANY

The First World War was fought mainly by large conscript armies. The concept of the 'citizen soldier' was established during the French Revolution and was based on the idea that all male citizens had a duty to bear arms in defence of their nation. Britain did not enforce conscription until January 1916 (see page 11), but **in Germany all able-bodied men aged 17-45 were liable for military service**. By 1914 the Germans had a well-established and organised system of peacetime conscription.

At the age of 20, men would undertake two or three years of peacetime training in the active army. At the end of their training they were allowed to go back into civilian life, but could be called back to the army at any time up to the age of 45.

Conscription meant that, by August 1914, **the German army needed just 12 days to expand from 800,000 to 3,500,000 soldiers**. In Germany, under 60% of military-aged men served. In 1916 Germany passed the Auxiliary Service Law, which made all men aged between 17 and 60 liable for service in some form, including war production.

DID YOU KNOW...?

MANY CHILDREN WERE UNABLE TO GET ENOUGH VITAMIN D IN THEIR DIET, WHICH LED TO WIDESPREAD BONE DEFORMATIONS AMONGST THE YOUNG.

BRITISH NAVAL BLOCKADE

One tactic that Britain used to help win the war was to starve Germany. They used their naval forces to cut off supplies coming from outside Germany in an attempt to starve the nation and force it to surrender. The Royal Navy blocked the entrance to the English Channel and the North Sea, and with the help of the French and Italians mounted another blockade in the Adriatic Sea, which affected Germany's ally, Austria-Hungary. The blockade, beginning at the start of the war and ending when Germany signed the Treaty of Versailles in June 1919, worked well. The naval forces successfully limited the supplies that reached Germany and its allies.

The consequences of the blockade were compounded by Germany's failure to manage its own food production effectively or to distribute food in ways that were equitable. Bad harvests in 1916 resulted in what the Germans called 'the turnip winter'. The country began to suffer from malnourishment, resulting in riots and starvation in some areas. The pattern was repeated in the winter of 1917–18. **After the war, Germany claimed that about one million people had died because of the blockade**, whether actually starving to death or contracting diseases such as tuberculosis and pneumonia.

GERMAN WAR ARTISTS

The work of German artists Kathe Kollwitz and Otto Dix reflected candidly on the world they saw falling apart around them. They both viewed their art as therapeutic for themselves and their society. They depicted images of war, grief and devastation, including starving children and soldiers with facial injuries.

Kathe Kollwitz: *The Survivors*, 1923.

KATHE KOLLWITZ (1867–1945)

Kathe Kollwitz was a German artist and sculptor, as well as an advocate for victims of social injustice, war and inhumanity. In 1914 her youngest son died in battle, hugely affecting her. **The way she felt best able to grieve was through her art**, and she produced many pieces on the theme of a mother protecting her children. In 1924, Kathe wanted to produce a memorial dedicated to her late son. She made two sculptures, *The Mother* and *The Father*, which were placed in a cemetery near Ypres where her son was buried.

OTTO DIX (1891–1969)

Otto Dix volunteered to join the military service at the beginning of the war. **He survived, but the horrors of the war stayed with him**. His paintings, influenced by Expressionism and Futurism, often reflected this. As a machine-gunner at the front, Otto experienced many of the gruesome parts of the First World War, which inspired his paintings. Due to Otto's graphic and disturbing depiction of the war and his 'mocking' of the German idea of heroism, he was dismissed from his teaching post at the Dresden Academy in 1933.

Storm Troopers Advancing Under Gas, 1924 by Otto Dix.

Some workers crucial to the war effort, particularly those in agriculture and munitions manufacturing, were exempt from military service.

RUSSIA

In 1914, Russia had an alliance with Serbia and so when Austria-Hungary invaded Serbia following the assassination of Archduke Franz Ferdinand, Russia mobilised its army. Germany declared war on Russia on 1st August 1914 (see page 8). Many Russians were hungry, poor and desperate for something to change; this was only increased by the First World War. Eventually the public turned against their Tsar, Nicholas II, and focus shifted from the Great War to Revolution.

THE BATTLE OF TANNENBERG

The Battle of Tannenberg, starting on 26th August 1914, was one of the largest battles on the Eastern Front during the First World War. It was fought in the German village Tannenberg, (now north-eastern Poland) and was a serious defeat for Russia.

Two Russian armies, commanded by General Paul von Rennenkampf (Pavel Karlovich Rennenkampf) and General Alexander Samsonov, invaded East Prussia, Germany, at the end of August 1914. One problem these two armies faced was poor communication. Not only was it extremely difficult to contact all the soldiers, as there was so many spread out so far, but also they were not careful enough with their radio communications! The Germans were able to listen in to the radio messages from each General, Rennenkampf stating that he was staying put and Samsonov that he was advancing.

Samsonov's route to invasion was difficult. The terrain was tough, his men were hungry and tired, and the Germans were expecting them! On 26th August the Russian army was surrounded and confused. On 29th August, Samsonov realised the hopelessness of the situation and took his own life. By 30th August his army no longer existed. The aftermath of this battle divided the nation.

War with Germany by Pavel Filonov (1883–1941), a Russian avant-garde painter and poet.

RUSSIAN REVOLUTION

There had been a revolution in Russia in 1905, and the country had not yet fully recovered from this when the Great War broke out in 1914. The early losses at the Battle of Tannenberg and also the First Battle of Masurian Lakes (around 125,000 casualties) increased tensions at home. **The public began to mistrust their leaders again, even accusing Tsarina Alexandra, wife to Tsar Nicholas, of being a German spy!**

With more money and men leaving the country, troubles and riots increased on the home front. In early 1917, a revolution overthrew Tsar Nicholas; however, the new government continued the war. There was a second revolution in October of the same year which brought the Bolshevik Party to power. The Bolsheviks agreed a ceasefire with Germany and signed the Treaty of Brest-Litovsk in March 1918.

NIKOLAI GUMILEV (1886–1921)

Nikolai was a Russian poet born in 1886 who fought at the front during the First World War as a volunteer. He was credited for his bravery and received two medals, including the distinguished Cross of St George. In 1916 he published a book of poems entitled *Kolchan* meaning 'The Quiver' which included a poem he wrote and published in 1914, *War*. In August 1921, **Nikolai was executed for acting against the Revolution and the Bolsheviks, even though there was no proof that he even disliked them!** Nikolai was married to Anna Akhmatova, who is often regarded as one of the greatest female poets in Russian literature. During the First World War she wrote about the impact of the Great War, Russia's own difficulties and the Russian Revolution. Anna and Nikolai divorced in 1918.

Война – *Nikolai Gumilev*

М. М. Чичагову

Как собака на цепи тяжёлой,
Тявкает за лесом пулемёт,
И жужжат шрапнели, словно пчёлы,
Собирая ярко-красный мёд.

А «ура» вдали, как будто пенье
Трудный день окончивших жнецов.
Скажешь: это — мирное селенье
В самый благостный из вечеров.

И воистину светло и свято
Дело величавое войны,
Серафимы, ясны и крылаты,
За плечами воинов видны.

Тружеников, медленно идущих
На полях, омоченных в крови,
Подвиг сеющих и славу жнущих,
Ныне, Господи, благослови.

Как у тех, что гнутся над сохою,
Как у тех, что молят и скорбят,
Их сердца горят перед Тобою,
Восковыми свечками горят.

Но тому, о Господи, и силы
И победы царский час даруй,
Кто поверженному скажет: — Милый,
Вот, прими мой братский поцелуй!

War – *Nikolai Gumilev*

M. M. Chichagov

A machine gun yelps beyond the trees,
like a dog on a heavy chain,
and shrapnel buzzes, like the sound of bees
collecting bright red honey.

From far away, one hears "Hurrah," just like the singing
of reapers when a hard day's done.
It all might seem like the most blessed evening
in a peaceful settlement.

Oh, yes, it is a deed that's bright and holy –
the majestic deed of waging war;
one sees the winged Seraphim so clearly
behind the men-at-arms.

I ask Thee now to grant Thy blessing, Lord,
to labourers who slowly make their way
across fields soaked with blood –
to bless the sowers' deeds, the reapers' glory.

Like those who bend above the wooden plough,
like those who pray, like those who mourn,
their hearts are fiery before Thee now –
their hearts, like candles, burn.

Yet I ask Thee, Lord, to grant both strength
and regal victory to one who says
to the defeated enemy: "My friend,
accept a brother's kiss!"

Translated by Boris Dralyuk

BELGIUM

Much of the fighting during the First World War took place on Belgian soil. More than 100,000 Belgians died during the war, and many others had their homes destroyed and fled the country.

FLANDERS FIELDS

From 1914 to 1918, Flanders Fields was a major battle theatre in the First World War. One million soldiers from more than 50 different countries were wounded, missing or killed in action there. **Ypres and Passchendaele became worldwide symbols for the great loss of life during the war**. The now-peaceful region still bears witness to this history in monuments, museums, cemeteries and the countless individual stories that link it with the world.

The Battlefield of Ypres was painted in 1919 by Scottish artist David Young Cameron (1865–1945).

THE GERMAN INVASION

At the very beginning of the war, the Germans wanted to march through Belgium in order to attack the French from the rear. They demanded that the Belgian King, Albert I, grant them passage through the country, but he refused. **On 4 August 1914, the German army invaded Belgium as part of the Schlieffen Plan**. The Plan was designed to bring a quick end to the war with a decisive German victory (see page 9).

On 12 August 1914 at Halen (a market town in the province of Limburg), Uhlans of the German cavalry (light cavalry armed with lances) attempted to charge a strong Belgian position with naked swords. This was unsuccessful, and the Belgians defended the town.

The German advance moved through Belgium much more slowly than the German High Command had originally hoped. At several places, the Germans believed that they were shot at by 'civilians'. The often incomplete uniform of the Belgian Civil Guard made it hard to recognise the soldiers. A large number of civilians were executed in retaliation in Dinant, Aarschot and Leuven. **In Leuven 2,000 houses and the**

The Cloth Hall, Ypres (1919) by Scottish painter Emily Murray Paterson (1855–1934) shows the ruined walls of the medieval building immediately after the end of the First World War.

university library were also burnt to the ground.

The fortress of Antwerp fell in October 1914. After the fall of Antwerp, the tired troops of the weakened Belgian Army withdrew behind the line of the River Yser. Trenches were dug, and the 'Yser Front' became part of the Western Front, a section that was held by the Belgians until 1918.

THE FLOODING OF THE YSER PLAIN

In October 1914, the German army launched an offensive aimed at breaking the Allied lines. They wanted to take Ypres and the roads leading to the Channel ports, meaning they would control the outlets to the North Sea. However, **the German advance was stopped when the Belgian Army deliberately flooded the Yser Plain**. At the same time, to the south, British and the French reinforcements successfully prevented a German breakthrough at Ypres.

THE MENIN GATE

Built in 1927, **the most famous Commonwealth War Memorial bears the names of 54,896 soldiers who were reported missing in the Ypres Salient between the outbreak of the war and 15th August 1917**. There was not enough space on the gate for soldiers reported missing after that date, so their names are listed on the wall of nearby Tyne Cot cemetery. An exception was made for Australian and Canadian soldiers who were missing in action until the end of the war. There are no New Zealand names, as their missing are commemorated in cemeteries near to where they died.

Every night at eight o'clock, the Last Post is played under the Menin Gate by the volunteers of the Ypres Last Post Association, who are members of the Ypres Voluntary Fire Brigade.

BELGIAN REFUGEES

Huge numbers of Belgians had their homes destroyed in the German invasion, and many people fled the country in the autumn of 1914. About 250,000 turned to Britain, and the War Refugees Committee (WRC) coordinated relief work to help them once they arrived. **The WRC asked the British public to help with accommodation, and within two weeks received 100,000 offers**. Local committees were set up, and charity events were organised all over the country.

Some refugees lived in purpose-built villages, which were considered Belgian territory, administered by the Belgian government and used Belgian currency. One of these communities was Elisabethville in Birtley, Tyne and Wear. However, most refugees were housed by families in all areas of England, Scotland, Wales and Ireland. Some remained in contact with the families long after the war ended.

Agatha Christie's famous detective Hercule Poirot was based on a Belgian refugee who stayed in her town, Torquay!

UNITED STATES OF AMERICA

The United States of America, under President Woodrow Wilson, maintained a policy of neutrality at the start of the war. However, this changed over time, and in April 1917 the US entered the war on the side of the Allies. Two million people from the US served in the military overseas during the First World War, including 200,000 naval personnel.

ENTERING THE WAR

At the beginning of the conflict, many people in the US believed that it was a 'European War' and that they should not get involved. However, **when a German U-Boat submarine sank the RMS *Lusitania* in May 1915, public opinion turned against Germany**.

The United States remained legally neutral, and President Wilson hoped they could act as a mediator to end the war. In 1916 Wilson ran for re-election on a platform of peace, and won with public support.

In 1917 Germany, desperate to end the War, began 'unrestricted submarine warfare', and in March sank five US ships. This shocked the public, and support for entering the war increased.

Congress declared war on Germany on 6th April 1917.

INDUSTRY

To fuel the Allied war effort, the US government mobilised industry to make weapons, equipment, munitions and supplies. This created new jobs and opportunities in the industrialising north.

Nearly one million women joined the workforce. Hundreds of thousands of African Americans from the south migrated north to work in factories. This meant that more Americans than ever were living in cities and working in manufacturing rather than in agriculture.

The government used propaganda to encourage people to buy government bonds and war savings stamps, and to work for the war effort.

The US contributed ammunition, supplies and machinery to the Allied forces after entering the war, which made a big difference to the outcome of the conflict.

Nearly 13,000 women joined the Navy as a Yeoman (F) and the Marines. More than 20,000 women served in the Army and Navy Nurse Corps.

MILITARY

Two million Americans volunteered for the army, and nearly three million were 'drafted' (conscripted). **Some volunteered to join the British forces before the US had even entered the War**.

More than 350,000 African Americans served in the First World War. At this time racial discrimination was legally enforced in the US, and African Americans were segregated from white troops in separate units.

The first contingent of the American Expeditionary Force (AEF) arrived in France in June 1917. They were commanded by General John J. Pershing, and under overall command of Marshall Foch of France. It took time to assemble, train and equip a fighting force. **By spring 1918, the AEF was ready, first halting a German offensive at the Battle of Belleau Wood**.

In August 1918, the US forces became independent from Marshall Foch's command, and the American First Army (AFA) was formed. The AFA pushed the enemy back at St Mihiel, and then moved north to join the Allies for the Meuse-Argonne Offensive (see page 122).

US propaganda and recruitment poster.

THE 1918 WORLD SERIES

In September 1918, the baseball World Series was due to be played in Chicago. This was the biggest baseball game in the US, and the Boston Red Sox were going to play the Chicago Cubs. The officials wanted to cancel the game out of respect for soldiers fighting in the war. But they soon found out that US troops were excited for the game and desperate for news of the result, so the game went ahead.

For the first time in any baseball game, the band played the new national anthem, 'The Star Spangled Banner', during the seventh-inning stretch of the game to honour the troops. All the spectators and players stood up to join in. Soon it became tradition to play 'The Star-Spangled Banner' at all baseball games and, eventually, nearly all sporting events. Red Sox supporters who were away from home were delighted to hear the news that their team had won.

The 1918 World Series became a focus for American patriotism.

IRELAND

Ireland was completely transformed by the First World War, and much of the country as we know it today was formed during and immediately after the conflict. Despite tensions between Britain and Ireland before the outbreak of war in 1914, there was widespread support for the British war effort and over 200,000 Irishmen from all walks of life and every part of the island served in the British forces, while Irish civilians played an important role on the home front.

PRE-WAR TENSIONS

In the early twentieth century, Ireland was an undivided country ruled by Britain; it was a part of the United Kingdom. Tensions over the introduction of Home Rule, a form of devolved government, had led to a militant response from members of the Irish Unionist community, who regarded themselves as British and opposed any steps that might weaken Ireland's link with the United Kingdom.

In 1912, 500,000 Unionists in Ulster, Ireland's northern province, signed a Covenant in protest against the introduction of the Third Home Rule Bill. In January 1913 the Ulster Volunteer Force (UVF) was formed, a paramilitary group dedicated to resisting the introduction of Home Rule. In response, Irish nationalists, who wanted some form of independence from Britain, formed the Irish Volunteer Force (IVF) in November. Members of the IVF swore to safeguard the introduction of Home Rule and were generally loyal to the nationalist Irish Parliamentary Party. When war broke out there were 180,000 members. The Irish Citizen Army (ICA) was formed in Dublin in November 1913 in response to police brutality during a bitter industrial dispute. The ICA was a small, well-trained socialist militia under the leadership of James Connolly and other trade unionists.

WARTIME SERVICE

In 1914, almost 30,000 Irishmen were serving in regiments of the regular British Army. Many served in Irish regiments such as the Royal Inniskillings and the Munster Fusiliers. A major Irish recruitment campaign was launched at the beginning of 1915, and the number of Irish volunteers remained quite steady until the end of war. Many volunteers were attached to one of three distinctly Irish divisions formed for wartime service: the 10th (Irish), the 16th (Irish) and the 36th (Ulster) divisions. **Over 210,000 Irishmen enlisted between 1914 and 1918 and served in every branch of the armed forces and in every theatre of war**. At least 35,000 Irishmen died as a result of military service.

Civilians on the Irish home front played a major role in the war effort. Dublin, Cork and Waterford became major centres of shell production, while over 37,000 workers were involved in war-related shipbuilding in Belfast. As in Britain, Irish women also took on jobs previously held by men, such as working in munitions factories; they also served as nurses for British civilian organisations or for the military Voluntary Aid Detachment.

DID YOU KNOW...?

AS MILITARY CONSCRIPTION WAS NEVER ENFORCED IN IRELAND, MOST IRISHMEN WHO SERVED DURING THE WAR WERE VOLUNTEERS.

THE BATTLE OF MESSINES

The Battle of Messines took place from 7th to 14th June 1917 with an aim to win the high ground in preparation for a major attack in August, the Third Battle of Ypres (Passchendaele) (see page 15). Aircraft worked closely with artillery units in the 10 days before the battle to weaken German defences ahead of the main attack, but the most effective tactic used by the Allies was the detonation of massive underground stores of high explosives via a network of tunnels under the ridge (for more on tunnelling, see page 19).

Overnight, the Allies bombarded the German troops with artillery. **In the early hours of 7th June, 19 mines were detonated under German trenches**. The explosions killed about 10,000 German troops and devastated the morale of the survivors. Within minutes of the detonations, nine Commonwealth divisions advanced towards German lines supported by tanks and gas shells (see page 16). Almost all objectives were achieved in the first three hours of the battle.

Two Irish divisions fought at Messines: the 16th (Irish) Division and the 36th (Ulster) Division. The 16th Division consisted mainly of Catholic officers and soldiers from nationalist communities, while the men of the 36th Division were mostly from Protestant communities in the north of the island with a strong sense of British identity. Although these men may have wanted different things for Ireland's future, they fought and died side by side at Messines ridge. The battle now has a special place in the Irish memory of the war.

Messines Ridge from Hill by George Edmund Butler (1872–1936), a British-born New Zealander.

"I'll go too!"

THE REAL IRISH SPIRIT.

Irish recruitment poster.

To learn more about Irish War Poets see pages 78 and 79.

SCOTLAND

Communities from every corner of Scotland were affected by the First World War as **more Scots per head enlisted and died in combat than in any other nation of the United Kingdom.** The 100,000 war dead were known as 'the Lost Generation'. For many young Scots, the opportunity to sign up with their friends as part of a Pals Battalion encouraged them to go to war. Scottish troops often led from the front, and are noted for their action at the battles of Arras, Cambrai and the Somme, and particularly for their action at the Battle of Loos in autumn 1915.

BATTLE OF LOOS

The Battle of Loos began on 25th September 1915, following a four-day artillery bombardment in which 250,000 shells were fired, and was referred to at the time as 'The Big Push'. Sir Douglas Haig led the offensive despite serious misgivings regarding the shortage of shells, lack of cover and the fatigued state of his troops. Battalions from every Scottish regiment took part in the battle, around 30,000 Scots in total.

Haig planned to use poison gas on the enemy to provide the British troops with cover from the German machine gunners; however, the plan backfired as the wind changed direction and blew the gas back on the British. **This was the first time the British Army used poison gas as a weapon**. Although in many parts of the battlefield the Germans had been pushed back, the British attack had lost the element of surprise, so the German machine-gunners mowed down the men in their thousands. The battle proved indecisive and of the 21,000 killed, over 7,000 were Scottish soldiers.

Waiting for the Wounded by Muirhead Bone.

THE RENT STRIKES

Thousands of workers migrated to munitions districts in areas of Glasgow in the early months of the First World War which meant the demand for housing rocketed. Many landlords in the area saw this as an opportune moment to increase rents in these districts. This was unpopular throughout the munitions districts, and so in February 1915 local women formed the Glasgow Women's Housing Association to resist rent rises. The first rent strike took place in spring of 1915 with around 25,000 tenants joining in. **With support from Lloyd George, the government introduced the Rent Restriction Act** which froze rent at 1914 levels.

> Bagpipe players were often the first to march 'over the top' piping the rest of the soldiers into battle.

SCOTTISH WOMEN'S HOSPITALS FOR FOREIGN SERVICE

The Scottish Women's Hospitals for Foreign Service (SWH) were founded in 1914 in response to female medical professionals having their services to the British Government rejected on the basis that the battlefield was 'no place for women'. With an acceptance from the French Government and financial support from the National Union of Women's Suffrage Societies and the American Red Cross the SWH opened its first Auxiliary hospital in Royaumont, France, under the French Red Cross.

Throughout the First World War the SWH arranged 14 medical units to serve in Corsica, France, Malta, Romania, Russia, Salonika (Thessaloniki) and Serbia.

Norah Neilson Gray (1882–1931): *The Scottish Women's Hospital: In The Cloister of the Abbaye at Royaumont. Dr Frances Ivens inspecting a French patient.*

CRAIGLOCKHART

Craiglockhart in Edinburgh was used as a specialist hospital to treat traumatised soldiers suffering from 'shell shock'. Several treatment methods were used to treat the patients, such as 'ergotherapy' and 'talking therapy'. Ergotherapy was an approach taken by Dr Arthur Brock which involved taking part in meaningful activities such as working in schools, and 'talking therapy' was advocated by Dr William Rivers who believed the best cure for psychological trauma was self-expression and social activity.

A whole cohort of well-known war poets passed through Craiglockhart including Siegfried Sassoon, Wilfred Owen, and Charles Hamilton Sorley. Dr Brock encouraged his patients to write poems for The Hydra magazine, the hospital's in-house publication. Around 80,000 soldiers were treated at Craiglockhart by the time the war ended in November 1918.

DID YOU KNOW...?

BY THE END OF 1915, THE BRITISH WERE ESTABLISHING SPECIAL SNIPER SCHOOLS. SOME OF THE FIRST INSTRUCTORS WERE GHILLIES, GAMEKEEPERS FROM THE SCOTTISH ESTATES. THEY TAUGHT MARKSMANSHIP, STEALTH AND CAMOUFLAGE.

CROWN DEPENDENCIES

The Crown Dependencies are the Bailiwick of Jersey, the Bailiwick of Guernsey and the Isle of Man. Jersey and Guernsey form part of the Channel Islands, an archipelago in the English Channel, and the Isle of Man lies in the Irish Sea to the west of mainland Britain. The isolated nature of these islands did not mean that they avoided the costs of war.

Although they were self-governing, both Jersey and Guernsey sent troops to the front and maintained Royal Militias which provided basic military training for young men. On the Channel Islands, 6,292 men from the Bailiwick of Jersey and 6,168 from the Bailiwick of Guernsey served during the First World War. Of those 12,460 men, 2,298 gave their lives.

JERSEY

General Kitchener's famous recruitment drive for Pals Battalions grabbed the attention of Jersey, and so the island set about forming its own unit. The Jersey Overseas Contingent of the Royal Jersey Militia, consisting of 230 men, went into active service with the 7th Battalion of the Royal Irish Rifles in March 1915. The Jerseymen spent much of 1915 training alongside the Irish volunteers and left for France in December of that same year.

Jerseymen fought at the Battle of Loos and the Somme in 1916, and at the Battle of Passchendaele in 1917. Having suffered severe casualties at Passchendaele, the remnants of the force fought at Cambrai which was their final action undertaken as part of the Royal Irish Rifles. The Jersey Company was part of the offensive that drove the enemy from the gates of Ypres at the end of September 1918.

The last members of the Jersey Company returned home in 1919. **One in four Jersey men who served during the war had died, while a similar number suffered serious wounds**. Jersey also housed prisoners of war: the site at Blanches Banques was home to 1,500 inmates and remained open until the autumn of 1919.

GUERNSEY

The first contingent of more than 240 men left the island in March 1915 and joined the 6th Battalion of the Royal Irish Regiment in 47 Brigade at Fermoy, Ireland.

By April 1916, men from Guernsey were manning parts of the trenches at Loos in France and were subject to a German attack which included the use of chlorine and tear gas. The Service Battalion of the Royal Guernsey Light Infantry was formed at the end of 1916 as a fighting force in its own right and trained in Guernsey and Kent. The Battalion saw action at the battles of Passchendaele and Cambrai, and later was tasked with defending the small town of Les Rues Vertes against a German counter-attack for two days where the unit suffered heavy casualties with around 40% of the regiment either killed or severely injured.

Guernsey also suffered a serious economic downturn due to a loss of tourism during the war years. A lack of manpower to support farming and the wider agricultural sector also severely impacted the island.

Inspection of the Regiment after the consecration the King's Colours of the Royal Guernsey Light Infantry at Montreuil, 1919.

THE ISLE OF MAN

The Isle of Man's booming tourist industry was severely affected by the First World War as many were nervous about the prospect of crossing the Irish Sea and coming into contact with German U-boats. This was exacerbated when the Royal Navy pressed into service 11 of the Isle of Man's Steam Packet Company's 15-strong fleet which left the island increasingly isolated from the outside world.

Under the Defence of the Realm Act (DORA) the British Government was able to move those it viewed as a threat to British interests to internment camps where large groups of people were confined without trial. These 'enemy aliens', as they were called, were usually citizens of hostile powers, namely those from Germany and Austria-Hungary. **The Isle of Man was selected to house the 'enemy aliens' in two internment camps**, one at Douglas – a requisitioned holiday camp – and the other a purpose-built camp at Knockaloe. The camp at Douglas held around 5,000 but it was Knockaloe that was the largest such camp in the British Isles; its population peaked in July 1916 at 22,769.

Records show that 8,261 men from the Isle of Man (Manx) enlisted in the armed forces, which translated into 82.3% of Manx men of military age joining the war effort. Of the more than 8,000 men who served, 269 of them received honours, 1,165 died and 987 were wounded.

George Kenner: *View of a PoW Camp, Isle of Man*, 1915–1919. A view looking down at the camp from a hillside, with a seated prisoner in the foreground. The camp stands in a valley and consists of rows of low huts surrounded by a high wire fence. On the hillside in the foreground prisoners in brown clothing appear to be at work, tending the gardens.

How do you think living on a small island would change your experience of war?

Why do you think islands like Jersey and the Isle of Man were selected as places to keep prisoners?

WALES

David Lloyd George, the Chancellor of the Exchequer, hoped that Wales would raise its own corps, as Canada and the ANZACs did. Recruiting in Wales did not go well enough to warrant such expectations, although it has been calculated that about 100,000 Welsh people had joined the army before May 1915. By the end of the War 272,000 Welshmen had fought and nearly 35,000 of them were killed. In South Wales, many men were employed as coal miners, undertaking work of vital national importance. Coal was used in the manufacture of steel for armaments and for the propulsion of both warships and merchantmen.

THE BATTLE OF MAMETZ WOOD

The 38th or Welsh Division (also known as Lloyd George's Division) aimed to capture Mametz Wood as part of the Battle of the Somme. Mametz Wood was the largest wood on the whole of the Somme battlefront. The 38th Division was made up of soldiers from many different Welsh regiments, such as the Royal Welch Fusiliers and the Welsh Regiment.

The Battle of Mametz Wood began 7th July 1916. The battle was expected to last for a matter of hours, but in fact went on for five days and the division suffered around 4,000 casualties. **The Welsh Division achieved their aim of driving back the Germans to their second line of defence by the end of the five days**.

HOME FRONT – WORKING WOMEN

The British Women's Institute (WI) was an organisation set up in response to the First World War, teaching women new skills in order to play an important part in their community. **The very first British branch was established in Wales, in Llanfairpwll, in 1915**. Although Welsh women played a vital part in cities and rural areas during the war, by the end they were expected to return to their traditional role as housewives. As a result, the numbers of working women in Wales fell. It was not until the Second World War that these women reasserted themselves once again.

A bardic name is a pseudonym used in Wales, Cornwall or Brittany by poets and other artists.

Fraternity (1920) by Augustus John (1878–1961). A scene with three soldiers standing amongst the rubble of a bombed building. Two of the soldiers, the one on the left looking much younger than the others, tilt their heads close together; they are sharing a light for their cigarettes.

HEDD WYN (1887-1917)

Ellis Evans enrolled at Trawsfynydd School in 1892 and is thought to have left around 1899 to work as a shepherd on the family farm. Ellis received a rich cultural education through the local Ebenezer Chapel and Sunday school. His father was a '*bardd gwlad*' (literally 'a country poet', this Welsh term refers to a poet who celebrates his community) and taught him to compose poetry. Ellis won his first prize for poetry at the age of 11.

In 1910, Ellis received the bardic name Hedd Wyn ('Blessed Peace') at a ceremony in Blanenau Ffestiniog. He competed in many local Eisteddfodau (which are competitive festivals of music and poetry held throughout Wales). The tone of Ellis's work, which had originally been influenced by nature and religion, changed after 1914 as he began to write about the horror of the war and his friends who had died on the battlefields.

When the government introduced conscription in 1916 Ellis enlisted with the 15th Battalion of the Royal Welch Fusiliers and trained at Litherland. **He set sail for France in June 1917 and was killed on the first day of the third battle of Ypres, 31 July 1917**. In September of the same year Ellis was posthumously awarded the bard's chair at the National Eisteddfod of Wales. The chair was draped in black cloth and has been known ever since as '*Y Gadair Ddu*' ('The Black Chair').

Rhyfel – *Hedd Wyn*

Gwae fi fy myw mewn oes mor ddreng,
   A Duw ar drai ar orwel pell ;
O'i ôl mae dyn, yn deyrn a gwreng,
   Yn codi ei awdurdod hell.

Pan deimlodd fyned ymaith Dduw
   Cyfododd gledd i ladd ei frawd;
Mae sŵn yr ymladd ar ein clyw,
   A'i gysgod ar fythynod tlawd.

Mae 'r hen delynau genid gynt
Yng nghrog ar gangau 'r helyg draw,
A gwaedd y bechgyn lond y gwynt,
   A'u gwaed yn gymysg efo'r glaw.

War – *Hedd Wyn*

Why must I live in this grim age,
   When, to a far horizon, God
Has ebbed away, and man, with rage,
   Now wields the sceptre and the rod?

Man raised his sword, once God had gone,
   To slay his brother, and the roar
   Of battlefields now casts upon
   Our homes the shadow of the war.

The harps to which we sang are hung
   On willow boughs, and their refrain
Drowned by the anguish of the young
   Whose blood is mingled with the rain.

Translated by Alan Llywd

THE BRITISH EMPIRE

When Britain declared war on Germany, it did so on behalf of the British Empire. There were four self-governing Dominions (Australia, Canada, New Zealand and South Africa) and close to 80 British colonies that fought in the First World War. Soldiers also came from Africa and South Asia (see pages 52–55). There was also a sizeable army from the Caribbean recruited into the British West Indies Regiment, which fought on the Western Front and in the Middle East.

GALLIPOLI

With troops mired in a seemingly endless stalemate on the Western Front, the British Cabinet decided to attack Germany's ally, the Ottoman Empire (today's Turkey) through the Dardanelles (see page 89). Britain hoped to take control of the important port of Constantinople (today's Istanbul), and reduce pressure on their Russian allies. **The Gallipoli peninsula was chosen for a three-pronged attack in April 1915, combining British, French, South Asian and ANZAC forces**.

The attack was initially successful, but Allied forces were stopped by an Ottoman defence that was masterminded by a German officer, Otto Liman von Sanders, and thus struggled to push beyond the beachhead. The ANZAC forces forged a reputation for themselves in fierce fighting north of the main beachheads, but still progress was slow. Another landing took place in August, but **even with reinforcements the Ottoman and German defence was too strong**. In the autumn it was decided that Gallipoli was too costly, and an evacuation was carefully planned. Troops left in stages and in secret, and distracted the enemy with games of cricket (see page 72).

The last of the force left the peninsula early in the morning of 9th January 1916.

Map of the eastern Mediterranean.

THE WEST INDIES

The West Indies donated sugar, rum, oil, lime, cotton, rice, clothing, logwood and nine aeroplanes to the British. A total of 11 ambulances and adequate funds for their maintenance were donated, and approximately two million pounds sterling was given to the British Government and charities.

Approximately 16,000 soldiers from the British West Indies Regiment (BWIR) saw action in France, Palestine, Egypt and Italy, and more than 1,000 other West Indians joined different regiments of the British Army. The British West Indies Regiment were all volunteers.

Men in the BWIR won 81 medals for bravery, and 49 were mentioned in dispatches. Around 1,500 soldiers from the British West Indies Regiment died during the war.

ANZAC stands for Australia and New Zealand Army Corps.

BATTLE FOR LAKE TANGANYIKA

The Allies aimed to take control of Lake Tanganyika as part of the East Africa Campaign in late 1915 (see page 52). The lake is the longest freshwater lake in the world and sits between Tanzania (then German East Africa) and the Democratic Republic of Congo (then the Belgian Congo). The German ship SMS *Graf von Goetzen* was able to move German troops along the lake, which made it difficult for the Allies to invade. The Germans also had two gunboats, the *Hedwig von Wissman* and the *Kingani*, patrolling the lake. **The Allies needed some armed motor launches (small vessels) to capture the lake. British vessels, HMS *Mimi* and HMS *Toutou*, had a long and strange journey from Britain to Lake Tanganyika, including rolling on logs whilst being pulled by oxen and steam tractors!**

The *Kingani* was captured on 26th December 1915, then repaired and renamed HMS *Fifi*. In January 1916, HMS *Mimi* and the newly captured HMS *Fifi* sank the *Hedwig*. These successes helped British and Belgian forces to advance overland into German East Africa. In July 1916, the Germans scuttled the *Goetzen* rather than let the ship fall into enemy hands. Once the British had control over Lake Tanganyika, the Belgians were able to pilot two planes loaned by Britain to bomb the Germans.

Local women carrying water for the traction engine hauling the motor launches *Mimi* and *Toutou* towards the Lake.

A soldier of the British West Indies Regiment rests during the digging of a new headquarters for XXth Corps on the cliffs of the Mediterranean near Deir el Belah, Palestine.

The Imperial War Cabinet was created in 1917 to coordinate the British Empire's military policy.

DID YOU KNOW...?

LOCAL WOMEN WALKED EIGHT MILES ONE WAY TO FETCH WATER FOR THE STEAM ENGINES TRANSPORTING HMS MIMI AND HMS TOUTOU ACROSS LAND. ONE TANK WOULD REQUIRE TWO TONNES OF WATER!

THE WAR IN THE MIDDLE EAST

GERTRUDE BELL (1868-1926)

Gertrude Bell was exceptionally bright; she was the first woman to gain a First Class Honours degree from Oxford University. She spoke multiple languages, including Arabic, Turkish and Persian, and had spent years in the Middle East. **It seemed that she had a more genuine understanding of the region's politics and culture than anyone else in the British government**.

When war broke out Gertrude begged to be sent to the Middle East, but the War Office said it was 'too dangerous for a woman'. Instead she was sent to Boulogne to run the Missing and Wounded Enquiry Department, which she did with huge success.

By 1915, Britain's policy in the Middle East was in disarray and the War Office belatedly decided to call on Gertrude. She was sent to Cairo with the rank of Military Intelligence Major (but not permitted to wear uniform) to work in the Arab Bureau. Her tasks were to map northern Arabia and to establish Arab leaders' loyalty to Britain. Her reports were crystal-clear and considered the best the Bureau had ever produced.

During the war, Gertrude sounded warnings that later proved accurate, but they were not taken on board at the time. In fact, it was she who first anticipated that chronic tensions between Sunni and Shi'a Muslims would ultimately spiral out of control.

THE BIKANER CAMEL CORPS

The Bikaner Camel Corps was led by the Maharaja of Bikaner, Ganga Singh. **The Maharaja and his soldiers patrolled the Sinai Desert mounted on camels, and were tasked to defend the Egyptian canals**. The Suez Canal was the only water route for supplies and troops between Asia and Europe, and the Sweet Water Canal was the main supply of drinking water for the Allied forces in the desert. In February 1916, the Corps was attacked by the Turkish Army, but successfully defended the canals and ensured the survival of the Allied forces. The Corps' counter-attack was led from the front by the Maharaja of Bikaner.

The Maharaja continued to be an important figure throughout the war, and when the conflict ended

The Bikaner Camel Corps.

he represented India at the peace negotiations. He was the only person of South Asian heritage to sign the Treaty of Versailles (see page 126).

LAWRENCE OF ARABIA (1888–1935)

Thomas Edward Lawrence, better known as Lawrence of Arabia, joined the British Army in late 1914 and was stationed in Cairo as an intelligence officer.

In 1916, Lawrence was sent to support the Arab Revolt. Under the command of General Sir Edmund Allenby, he and the Arab fighters rode hundreds of miles to attack the Ottoman Army where it least expected it, Aqaba, a port in the Red Sea. Rather than attacking from the coast, the direction from which the Turks could anticipate danger because of the British Navy, Lawrence decided to emerge from the Nefudh Desert. As Allenby's forces advanced into Palestine in 1917–18, **Lawrence and the Arabs severed the enemy's lines of communication from Turkey and destroyed the railway lines**.

After this success, the British government was keen to receive more help from the Arab Army under Lawrence's leadership. By the beginning of October 1918, both the British and the Arab armies were in Damascus, and within a month Ottoman Turkey had surrendered.

This famous portrait of Lawrence of Arabia was painted in 1918 by James McBey.

MESOPOTAMIA

After the Ottoman Empire entered the war, the British felt their interests in the Middle East were threatened. They wanted to protect their oil reserves and put pressure on the Ottomans, and so they deployed a force made up overwhelmingly of Indian troops to Mesopotamia (modern-day Iraq). **The British and Indian troops arrived there in November and were able to achieve a few early successes against the Turkish army, capturing the main port of Basra**. These successes gave the Allies the confidence to push on to Baghdad. However, the Ottomans checked General Townshend's Anglo-Indian force at Ctesiphon, an ancient city to the south of Baghdad, and Townshend was forced to retreat to Kut. The Turks besieged the town, and efforts to relieve the garrison failed. In April 1916, Townshend surrendered. Britain made better preparations and took Baghdad in 1917. By the war's end, they had reached as far north as Mosul.

Forced Landing in Mesopotamia by Sydney Carline (1888–1929).

You can visit the Imperial Camel Corps Memorial in London's Victoria Embankment.

THE WAR IN AFRICA

When war broke out between the Entente and the Central Powers, their colonies were immediately drawn in. Africa donated 274 planes, and hundreds of thousands of men from Africa fought for the British during the First World War – it is difficult to know the exact numbers, since records are still being transcribed. The term 'African' used here includes Blacks, Whites, Indians, Coloureds and Arabs. Many died of disease and malnutrition. An estimated 10% died from direct war causes. African troops were awarded 166 decorations for bravery.

EAST AFRICA CAMPAIGN

The East Africa Campaign was one theatre of conflict where the Germans had not already surrendered by the time of the Armistice. The campaign began on 8th August 1914 and ended on 25th November 1918.

The East African Front included South Africans, Germans Belgians and Portuguese, as well as Africans from across the continent. There were at least 177 'micro-nations' also involved. **The fighting took place over 750,000 square miles, and seven territories were directly involved in the fighting**. They were: Belgian Congo (Democratic Republic of Congo), British East Africa (Kenya), German East Africa (Tanzania, Rwanda and Burundi), Northern Rhodesia (Zambia), Nyasaland (Malawi), Portuguese East Africa (Mozambique) and Uganda.

One important naval battle in East Africa was the sinking of the *Königsberg* ship in the Rufiji Delta. The British were determined to destroy the ship because it was such a threat to their sea lanes in the Indian Ocean, but found it difficult to locate. When the ship was found, the battle was slow but the British succeeded and the Germans ordered the *Königsberg* to be scuttled.

The biggest threat to soldiers' health in Africa was the environment. Many died because of disease and lack of food.

Men of the 1/4th King's African Rifles (KAR) at Njombe, German East Africa. Formed at the beginning of the century from tribesmen in British East Africa (now Kenya) and Uganda, the KAR bore the brunt of the fighting during the campaign.

WEST AFRICA

British West Africa included Nigeria, the Gold Coast (today's Ghana), Sierra Leone and The Gambia. The soldiers of the British colonies were divided into two military formations, the West African Regiment in Sierra Leone and the **West African Frontier Force (WAFF)**. Both of these were led by British officers. **At the beginning of the war, the WAFF had over 8,000 soldiers, of whom less than 400 were British and over 5,000 were Nigerian**.

Early on in the war, the British decided to destroy all wireless stations in German colonies. The first station they destroyed was in Kamina, Togo, which had enough power to relay communications between all Germany's African colonies and its cruisers in adjacent waters to Berlin. The German force lacked local support

German claims in Africa according to historian Hans Delbrück (1917).

and had only 300 German and 1,200 native troops. After capturing Lomé on 7th August 1914, the British and French advanced towards Kamina. **By 25th August, the Germans had surrendered and set fire to Kamina rather than letting it fall into the hands of the Allies**.

> Some soldiers were dragged out of their tents by lions!

SOUTHERN AFRICA

British troops were stationed in the Union of South Africa prior to the start of the First World War. Just a few weeks after the outbreak of war, South Africa took over its defence, and British troops were re-stationed in European combat zones, leaving a small number of officers behind.

Over 146,000 men served in South African units during the war. The most significant military campaign in Southern Africa was the South African invasion of German South-West Africa (today's Namibia). **South African units also fought on the Western Front, in Egypt, Palestine and in the East Africa Campaign**.

In 1915, the lack of water in South-West Africa caused major problems for the South African forces. For instance, after the South Africans took control of the port of Swakopmund they began to advance on Windhoek. When they arrived there, they found that the Germans had put signs up to say that they had poisoned the wells. German forces were keen to avoid large-scale battles in order to prolong the campaign.

The South African fighting contingent consisted mainly of white soldiers, with black auxiliaries acting in supporting roles and about 2,450 South Africans who served in the Royal Flying Corps.

DID YOU KNOW...?

THE EQUIVALENT OF TRENCH FOOT ON THE AFRICAN FRONT WAS THE JIGGER FLEA. THE FLEAS WOULD LAY EGGS IN SOLDIERS' TOES!

SOUTH ASIA

Over a million South Asian men* served in the Indian Army during the First World War. These soldiers came from modern-day Bangladesh, Bhutan, Burma, India, Nepal, Pakistan and Sri Lanka. In 1914, Bangladesh, Burma, India and Pakistan were all called India. As well as troops, India contributed 170,000 animals (including horses, camels and mules), 3.7 million tonnes of supplies and stores (including military hardware, cotton and grains), and by 1918–19 its total net military expenditure amounted to £121.5 million.

ACTIVE SERVICE

Muslims, Sikhs and Hindus all fought during the War and saw active service as infantrymen, cavalrymen and in non-combatant roles. South Asian men served in France, Belgium, Gallipoli, Mesopotamia (see page 51) and East Africa (see page 52). Troops of the Indian Army made up half the attacking force at the Battle of Neuve Chapelle in 1915.

This painting by James McBey depicts the Wadi Ali, one of the three passes by which access to the Judaean Plateau is possible. A large mass of British and Indian Army troops move across a flat plain leading to a narrow mountain pass. On the left an artillery gun is pulled by a tractor, with a train of camels on the right.

Sepoy, 14th Sikhs by John Daniel Revel (1884–1967).

WRITING HOME

Most South Asian soldiers were unable to read or write, so their own letters were usually written for them by scribes, and those they received were read to them out loud. **The British Army had a team of censors who monitored letters being sent home, but the soldiers quickly worked this out and resorted to coded language.** Most codes were deciphered fairly easily; however, some more subtle ones would have eluded the censors. The chief censor produced a weekly report in which he made general comments on the contents of the letters.

*Records of the number of Indian personnel involved range between 1-1.5 million

SAROJINI NAIDU (1879-1949)

Sarojini Naidu was a distinguished poet who spent much of her life campaigning for Indian independence. **She was known as 'the Nightingale of India' and was the first Indian woman to be president of the National Congress**. *The Gift of India* reflects Sarojini's love for her country, and reminds us of the sacrifices made during the First World War.

RECRUITMENT

The British Indian Army tried to recruit from areas where they believed men were better suited to war. **They preferred men from hilly, colder regions, such as the Gurkhas, Punjabi Sikhs and Muslims, and Rajputs from what is now northern India**. They called people from these regions the 'martial races'.

Men whom the British did not view as 'martial races' served in non-combatant roles. They ensured that food, water, and medical supplies arrived to the front line, and faced danger and death just like the fighting soldiers. About 600,000 South Asians served as non-combatants. These included the Supply and Transport Corps, the Bengal Ambulance Corps and the Pioneer units.

The British Indian Army remained a volunteer army; conscription was never introduced. However, some recruiting parties used harsh measures to gain recruits.

The Gift of India – *Sarojini Naidu*

Is there ought you need that my hands withhold,
   Rich gifts of raiment or grain or gold?
Lo! I have flung to the East and the West
Priceless treasures torn from my breast,
And yielded the sons of my stricken womb
To the drum-beats of the duty, the sabers of doom.
   Gathered like pearls in their alien graves
   Silent they sleep by the Persian waves,
   Scattered like shells on Egyptian sands,
They lie with pale brows and brave, broken hands,
they are strewn like blossoms mown down by chance
On the blood-brown meadows of Flanders and France
   Can ye measure the grief of the tears I weep
   Or compass the woe of the watch I keep
   Or the pride that thrills thro' my heart's despair
And the hope that comforts the anguish of prayer?
   And the far sad glorious vision I see
   Of the torn red banners of victory?
when the terror and the tumult of hate shall cease
   And life be refashioned on anvils of peace,
   And your love shall offer memorial thanks
To the comrades who fought on the dauntless ranks,
And you honour the deeds of the dauntless ones,
   Remember the blood of my martyred sons!

AUSTRALIA

In 1901, the six separate colonies of Australia united to form the Commonwealth of Australia. Australia was a Dominion of the British Empire whose population was made up of indigenous Aboriginals and others from European, mainly British, lineage. It has been reported that the outbreak of war was met with great enthusiasm from the Australians, with their Prime Minister, Andrew Fisher, declaring that Australia would support Britain to 'the last man and the last shilling'. Despite several unsuccessful attempts to introduce conscription through referendums held in 1916 and 1917, enlistment remained strictly voluntary throughout the war – over 400,000 Australian men enlisted.

ANZAC

The Australians saw action early on in the war with the Australian Naval and Military Expeditionary Force taking possession of German New Guinea on 17th September 1914 and the neighbouring islands of the Bismarck Archipelago (the Islands Region of Papua New Guinea) in October 1914. The Australians' most famous engagement was during the failed invasion of Gallipoli in 1915 (see page 48) – this campaign was considered the 'birth of a nation' for both Australia and New Zealand. **The Gallipoli campaign included 50,000 Australians and 9,000 New Zealanders**, who suffered around 8,700 and 2,700 casualties respectively.

The day of the invasion, 25th April, was officially named ANZAC Day in 1916 and was marked by a variety of ceremonies and services, including a commemorative march through London involving Australian and New Zealand troops. ANZAC Day is commemorated annually around the world with a dawn service and has become the focal point for how we remember Australia and New Zealand during the First World War.

The Battle of the Landings – ANZAC – Night, 25th April 1915 by Herbert Hillier. Crew members of HMS *Manica* stand on the deck of the ship trying to view developments on the shore at Anzac Cove on the western side of the Gallipoli peninsula.

This is an Australian adaptation of the soldier-song
'Take Me Back to Dear Old Blighty'

Take me back to dear old Aussie,

Put me on the boat for Woolloomooloo.

Take me over there, drop me anywhere,

Sydney, Melbourne, Adelaide, for I don't care.

I just want to see my best girl,

Cuddling up again we soon will be;

O Blighty is a failure, take me back to Australia,

Aussie is the place for me.

MULTIPLE FRONTS

Australian forces fought all over the world, including at sea with the Royal Australian Navy (RAN) and in the air with the Australian Flying Corps.
Following the Gallipoli campaign, the Australians fought campaigns on the Western Front and in the Middle East. They also saw action in many of the campaigns along the Western Front, including the Somme and Passchendaele. They suffered greatly, particularly at the Battle of Fromelles on 19th–20th July 1916, during which the Australians suffered 5,500 casualties overnight on what was described as the worst day ever in Australian history.

In the Middle East, the Australians fought a mobile war, unlike their counterparts on the Western Front, and had to endure extreme heat, harsh terrain and water shortages. The Australian forces participated in the Allied reconquest of Egypt's Sinai Peninsula in 1916, the advancement into Palestine to capture Gaza and Jerusalem in 1917, and the occupation of Lebanon and Syria in 1918 that resulted in Turkey suing for peace on 30th October 1918.

AUSTRALIAN ARMY NURSING SERVICE

The Australian Army Nursing Service (AANS) was formed in 1903 as part of the Australian Army Medical Corps. It was a reserve unit, and during the First World War more than 2,000 of its members served overseas alongside Australian nurses working with other organisations. **Australian tolerance for high temperatures made them particularly well suited for climates in Greece (where the wounded from Gallipoli were treated), Egypt and India.** The nurses were posted to the 1st Australian General Hospital (1AGH), established in the grand Heliopolis Palace Hotel in Cairo, or to 2AGH in Mena House, a former royal hunting lodge. There was a rapid influx of patients from Gallipoli in April 1915, which meant that these two hospitals in Egypt quickly became overcrowded. 1AGH took over an amusement park, turning the ticket office into an operating theatre, and the skating rink, scenic railway and skeleton house into wards. Within three months it was operating as a 1,500-bed hospital.

> The Australian Imperial Force (AIF) was formed on 15th August 1914 as a new overseas force. It initially included one infantry division and one light horse brigade.

Troops of the 1st Australian Division at dinner, Fleurbaix, France, May 1916.

NEW ZEALAND

Although best known for fighting at Gallipoli as part of the ANZAC troops (see page 56), New Zealand played a vital and varied role in the war. Around 18,000 New Zealanders died in or because of the war, and there were 41,000 instances of wounding or illness. In 1914, New Zealand had a population of just over one million; and by the end of the war, one in every four New Zealand men aged 20–45 was either killed or injured.

FIGHTING

Of the 250,000 men in New Zealand who were of eligible age to fight, 100,000 served overseas in the New Zealand Expeditionary Force (NZEF). This included more than 2,200 Māori and around 500 Pacific Islanders, mainly from the Cook Islands and Niue. Conscription was introduced in 1916 by the Military Service Act, and the men who were called up to fight served alongside volunteers.

The New Zealand Native Contingent was composed of Māori troops. They were attached to the New Zealand Mounted Rifles Brigade and took part in the August Offensive at Gallipoli. **When the command was given to charge, the soldiers burst into chants of 'Ka mate, ka mate!', terrifying men in the Turkish trenches**. The Pacific Islands offered troops to the British as soon as war broke out, but the offers were not accepted until after 1915, when the New Zealand forces were seriously depleted. When Niuean

Visit of New Zealand Prime Minister William F Massey and deputy prime minister Sir Joseph Ward to the Western Front, 30th June–2nd July 1918. Men of the New Zealand (Maori) Pioneer Battalion perform a haka for the dignitaries at Bois de Warnimont, 30 June 1918.

soldiers were sent to the Western Front, 82% were hospitalised with Western illnesses. After this, Pacific Islanders of the Rarotongan Company were sent to Sinai and Palestine to support the British, where they did vital work handling ammunition.

DID YOU KNOW...?

10,000 HORSES FROM NEW ZEALAND WENT TO WAR WITH THE NZEF! NEW ZEALAND HORSES WERE CONSIDERED TO BE VERY STURDY AND RELIABLE, AND THE NEW ZEALAND VETERINARY CORPS WORKED HARD TO LOOK AFTER THEM.

Red Cross poster to raise funds to aid sick and wounded soldiers.

NEW ZEALAND ARMY NURSING SERVICE

The New Zealand Army Nursing Service (NZANS) was established by Heather Maclean, who went with five other nurses to provide medical support to the NZEF force that captured German Samoa (see page 28). The Government were unwilling to allow women to serve overseas. Maclean received huge numbers of applications from other women to enlist and demanded that they be allowed to serve. Eventually, the Government allowed her to take nurses overseas. **The nurses faced judgements from the British about being 'colonials', but quickly proved themselves to be better trained, more flexible, and better able to cope with the climate than most nurses from England.**

Throughout the war, about 550 New Zealand women served in the NZANS. This included working on hospital ships (see page 112), at Gallipoli, on the Western Front, and at New Zealand hospitals in England.

HOME FRONT

Many people were supportive of involvement in the War in 1914, and remained generally assured of eventual victory throughout the war. Huge numbers of casualties at the Battle of Passchendaele lowered morale.

New Zealanders at home held Queen Carnivals to raise money for the forces. Women competed for the title of Queen in their local area and charged money for votes. Women of all ages took part, and claimed the crown based on their wit, intelligence, beauty and patriotism. There were also concerts, fêtes, bazaars and lotteries to raise money. Although some people felt that in the face of grief and suffering these were inappropriate, the fund-raisers were very effective at collecting money, and many people found them a positive distraction from the difficulties of war.

News of the war took weeks to reach the island of Niue, but once word arrived it took just 24 hours for the island to offer troops and raise money for the New Zealand Red Cross!

100 women from New Zealand travelled to Europe and enlisted as nurses with British or French nursing organisations.

CANADA

When Britain declared war in 1914, Canada was automatically drawn in as a Dominion of the British Empire. Canada had a small army of about 3,000 soldiers, and so the federal government, under Prime Minister Robert Borden, formed the Canadian Expeditionary Force (CEF) of about 35,000 men. Around 630,000 Canadians served in the CEF throughout the First World War.

The Taking of Vimy Ridge, Easter Monday, 1917 by Richard Jack (1866–1952), the first official Canadian war artist.

BATTLE OF VIMY RIDGE

The Battle of Vimy Ridge started on 9th April 1917 and was the first time all four Canadian divisions fought together. German forces captured Vimy Ridge in October 1914 and transformed it into a strong defensive position. They had built a complex system of tunnels and trenches manned by highly trained soldiers with machine guns and artillery pieces. The Canadian Corps was commanded by General Julian Byng who, after learning from mistakes made at the Battle of the Somme, prepared his soldiers with intense training that helped them to make quick decisions. The soldiers were also assisted by maps drawn up from aerial photographs and deep tunnels dug from the rear to the front by engineers. On the first day of battle, around 15,000 Canadians rose from the trenches, while nearly 1,000 guns opened fire on German positions.

It was a difficult battle but **the Canadians captured most of the Ridge on the first day, and the remaining positions were all taken by 12th April**. The success for the Allies came at a cost; more than 10,000 soldiers were killed or wounded.

THE CANADIAN PATRIOTIC FUND

Sir Herbert Ames established the Canadian Patriotic Fund (CPF) in August 1914. The organisation took donations during and after the war from many individuals and businesses wanting to support the Canadian soldiers and their families. The idea was to reassure the married soldiers going overseas to fight, which was 20% of all Canadian soldiers during the war. These soldiers were promised that in their absence their wives and families would be cared for and supported. Most Canadians believed it was their duty to support their soldiers' families, but the CPF still urged many to donate, encouraging Canadians to fight or to pay.

Canadian propaganda poster.

After The Speeches About The Empire
Ted Plantos (1943-2001)

I remember the Union-Jack-waving crowds

Before our train pulled out, and the quiet later

That choked their gaiety – how they went black

And motionless white when the last photograph was taken

I volunteered with twenty-one others

August of '14 it was, and we were handsome then

In our red tunics, trousers as blue

As the ocean we ached to cross

And white helmets marching to the railway station

Sam Hughes couldn't have hoped for more

They were joining up right across Canada

In Vancouver we burned the Kaiser in effigy,

Soaked him in kerosene and applauded the flames

The crowds cheered us in our new uniforms

When we marched ahead of automobiles,

Horses and buggies and the local fire brigade

Loaded down with flags

One of the officers told me

The war would last only three months,

And I'd likely not see any action

After the speeches about the Empire

Soaked up our hearts and were over,

The band played 'God Be With You Till We Meet Again'.

And the crowded platform

Went motionless quiet

When the train with us out the windows pulled away.

Source: Colombo, John Robert, and Michael Richardson, *We Stand on Guard: Poems and Songs of Canadians in Battle*, Toronto: Colombo & Company, 1998.

DID YOU KNOW...?
THE CANADIAN FORESTRY CORPS CUT AND PREPARED TIMBER IN EUROPE FOR THE ALLIED WAR EFFORT.

FARMING

The government were aware of the agricultural labour shortage, and in an effort to boost employment of women and children they formed the Farm Service Corps 'Farmerettes'. The Farmerettes were involved in all types of farm work, often replacing men who had joined the military. The programme existed only in the Ontario province, and **in 1918 there were 2,400 women picking fruit in the Niagara region**.

Prior to the start of the war, many rural women were part of the agricultural labour force. The war years were particularly challenging for them without the support from their husbands and sons. Canadian women contributed significantly to allied food production, especially of wheat.

The famous war poem 'In Flanders Fields' was written by Canadian military doctor and artillery commander, Major John McCrae.

DID YOU KNOW...?
CANADA'S NATIONAL PROGRAMME 'SOLDIERS OF THE SOIL' HAD A SIMILAR PURPOSE TO THE FARMERETTES, BUT WAS AIMED AT ADOLESCENT BOYS. IT RECRUITED 22,385 YOUNG MEN FROM ACROSS THE COUNTRY!

COMMONWEALTH WAR GRAVES COMMISSION

HISTORY OF THE COMMISSION

The Commonwealth War Graves Commission (CWGC) owes its existence to the vision and determination of one man – Sir Fabian Ware. At 45, Ware was too old to fight, but he became commander of a mobile unit of the British Red Cross. He noted that there was no organisation in place to record the final resting place of casualties, and became concerned that graves would be lost forever, so his unit took it upon themselves to register and care for all the graves they could find. By 1915, their work was given official recognition by the War Office and incorporated into the British Army as the Graves Registration Commission.

On 21st May 1917, his diligence was recognised when the Imperial (now Commonwealth) War Graves Commission was established by Royal Charter with Ware as its Vice-Chairman.

After the war, **Sir Fabian Ware explained his motivation saying, 'Common remembrance of the dead [of the Great War] is the one thing, sometimes the only thing, that never fails to bring our people together'.**

THE COMMISSION TODAY

The Commonwealth War Graves Commission still cares for memorials to honour and commemorate the 1.7 million people who died in the two world wars.

CWGC cemeteries, burial plots and memorials are a lasting tribute to those who died, and can be found at almost 23,000 locations in 153 different countries around the world.

The cost of the work is shared by the member governments – Australia, Canada, India, New Zealand, South Africa and the United Kingdom – in proportions based on the number of their graves.

More than 130,000 of those commemorated in the UK have no known grave but are remembered by name on memorials to the missing.

CWGC

Commonwealth War Graves Commission

EQUALITY OF COMMEMORATION

The Commission honours all casualties equally, without distinction on account of rank, race or creed. Individual graves are marked by headstones, which are all identical except for their inscriptions: the national emblem or regimental badge, rank, name, unit, date of death and age of each casualty are inscribed above an appropriate religious symbol and a more personal dedication chosen by relatives.

INTERPRETING A HEADSTONE

National Emblem or Unit/Regimental badge
Originally, the headstones were carved by hand; now all headstones are made by computer-aided machinery. Details of the individual will normally include the military number, rank, military awards, regiment, age and date of death.

Religious Emblem
Most CWGC headstones include a religious icon, like the Christian cross, Jewish or Muslim emblems.

Personal Inscription
Graves were made more individual by personal inscriptions. With a limit of 66 letters, the words chosen were often religious or messages of loss from the family.

COMMANDANT KATHERINE HARLEY

Commandant Katherine Mary Harley led a group of nurses of the Scottish Women's Hospital (see page 43) serving with the Serbian Army. Her brother was Field Marshal Sir John French, Commander-in-Chief of the BEF in France and Flanders in 1914–1915. Mrs Harley was killed in the bombing in Serbia. She was typical of the many women who served with the nursing and similar forces of the Commonwealth, and whose graves lie wherever those forces served. She is buried in CWGC's Salonika (Lembet Road) Military Cemetery in Thessaloniki. Her grave bears a private memorial erected in 1917 by the Serbian Army and inscribed in two languages:

The generous English lady and great benefactress of the Serbian people, Madame Harley, a great lady. On your tomb instead of flowers the gratitude of the Serbs shall blossom there for your wonderful acts. Your name shall be known from generation to generation.

The Memorial to Katherine Mary Harley in Thessaloniki, Greece.

DID YOU KNOW...?

DURING THE FIRST WORLD WAR, THERE WAS A PRACTICE OF NON-REPATRIATION OF THE DEAD. THIS MEANT THAT COMMONWEALTH PERSONNEL WERE BURIED OR CREMATED WHERE THEY DIED, SO MAJOR BATTLEFIELDS REMAIN CEMETERIES TO THIS DAY.

To find out more please visit:
www.cwgc.org

COMMONWEALTH WAR GRAVES COMMISSION

IN THE UK

As part of their efforts, the CWGC maintains a database of all the Commonwealth forces who lost their lives during the two wars. The entire database is available at www.cwgc.org, and can be easily searched, allowing you to locate any of your ancestors who may have died in the conflicts.

There are more than 300,000 Commonwealth war dead commemorated in the United Kingdom – in almost 13,000 locations. This is the highest total of world war commemorations in any country other than France.

Most people whose graves are in the UK died in military hospitals from wounds. Others may have died in training accidents or air raids, and some were killed in action in the air or at sea in coastal waters, where their bodies washed ashore. For most, the UK was their home.

Some of the graves are concentrated in large war cemeteries, but most are in cemeteries containing 10 or fewer war graves. Sometimes the war graves are grouped together, but often they are scattered throughout the cemetery. This is because wartime service burials were not strongly regulated for those who died in their own country, so many were laid to rest in locations chosen by their families, instead of in war cemeteries.

The CWGC Military Cemetery in Brookwood, Surrey.

TAKING PART

For support with organising a school visit to your local CWGC site, email community@cwgc.org

You can search for war casualties by name, location and/or regiment with the CWGC database online at www.cwgc. org, and use it to research your local war graves before visiting them.

DID YOU KNOW...?

IN THE CWGC THERE ARE THOUSANDS OF PEOPLE WHO DO IMPORTANT WORK TO KEEP GRAVES LOOKING AS THEY SHOULD. FROM GARDENERS TO STONE REPAIR TECHNICIANS AND REGIONAL OFFICERS, MANY PEOPLE PLAY THEIR PART IN MAKING SURE THE GRAVES ARE MAINTAINED PROPERLY.

CWGC
Commonwealth War Graves Commission

FINDING A LOCAL CASUALTY FROM THE FIRST WORLD WAR

When the First World War came to an end in November 1918, war graves were scattered throughout all of the regions where fighting had occurred. The locations and sites of many graves were no longer known, and individuals still lay, unburied, in areas where fighting had been fiercest.

Where burials had occurred in established burial grounds, with clearly marked graves, the graves were simply recorded and registered. In most other cases, the bodies had to be exhumed and reburied. During this process, CWGC attempted to identify the bodies. Old battlefields were searched for casualties, and small cemeteries were concentrated into larger ones. Names of the missing were collected from military authorities, and engraved onto memorials.

The CWGC began to collect a huge amount of information about all the individuals who had died. All of these documents were created in the pre-computer age, and the grave registration and concentration records were usually typed up from hand-written reports produced in the field, in all types of weather and conditions.

The database is now a lot easier to use and understand – it is available online, and you can use it to find the records of anyone commemorated by a CWGC grave or memorial. You can search for a surname, and records from all Commonwealth nations are accessible.

Do you think it's important to memorialise fallen soldiers? Why?

NUMBER OF WAR DEAD BY FORCES

	Identified Burials	Commemorated on Memorials
United Kingdom & Colonies	478,648	409,584
Undivided India	8,097	66,099
Canada	45,495	19,499
Australia	38,796	22,284
New Zealand	11,761	6,292
South Africa	6,684	2,854

To find out more, please visit:
www.cwgc.org

COMMONWEALTH STORIES

MANTA SINGH

Died: 30.03.1915
Commemorated: Patcham Down Indian Forces Cremation Memorial, Sussex

Manta Singh was born in 1870 near Jalandhar, Punjab, northern India. As soon as he left school, he joined the 15th Ludhiana Sikhs, an infantry regiment of the Indian Army. At the start of the First World War, the regiment became part of the 3rd (Lahore) Division, sent to reinforce the BEF fighting in France.

After long months of trench warfare, in March 1915, Manta Singh's regiment prepared to engage in the Battle of Neuve Chapelle, in which half of the Commonwealth fighting force, 20,000 men, were Indian Army soldiers.

On 10th March, four divisions, comprising 40,000 men, gathered on a sector of the front which was less than two miles wide. The infantry attack was preceded by heavy but concentrated shelling from 342 guns, guided by reconnaissance planes of the Royal Flying Corps.

During an attempt by British soldiers to take Aubers River, Manta Singh witnessed an English comrade, Captain Henderson, sustain a serious injury. Manta pushed him to safety in a wheelbarrow he found in No Man's Land, but he himself was severely injured while carrying out this selfless rescue.

Manta and his wounded comrades were shipped to England, where hospitals had been set up to meet their needs. Here, sadly, his wounds became infected with gangrene. He was told his legs would have to be amputated to save his life, a thought which filled him with despair. He died from blood poisoning a few weeks later.

COLOUR SERGEANT GEORGE WILLIAMS

Died: July 1918

Colour Sergeant George Williams, 1/3rd Regiment Kings African Rifles (KAR), was a Sudanese soldier with an English name. He was awarded the KAR Distinguished Conduct Medal (DCM) for reconnaissance work at Tsavo, East Africa in September 1914.

The following year, in January 1915 at Jassin in the Umba Valley, Colour Sergeant Williams, while under heavy enemy fire, extricated the remainder of his platoon after one officer (Lieutenant GM Dean 1/3rd KAR) had been killed and another seriously wounded. Colour Sergeant Williams also managed personally to carry away the platoon machine gun after the crew and

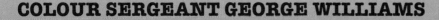

supporting carriers had all been killed or wounded too.

For this deed, the Divisional Commander Major MJ General Tighe, recommended Williams for the Victoria Cross (VC). If this award had been approved, George Williams would have been the first soldier in the KAR to be so honoured. He did not receive the VC, but he was eventually awarded a bar to his DCM before he was killed later in July 1918. The main reason that the VC was not confirmed would seem to be inter-departmental politics. The War Office was not going to have the Colonial Office handing out their highest military decoration.

The Battle of Jutland (1920) is an oil painting on canvas by Robert Henry Smith.

Marcus Bailey was born in Barbados in 1884, but later lived in Liverpool.

Bailey served as a Merchant Seaman in the Royal Navy from 1903. He married Lilian in 1913, and when war broke out in the following year he went to serve at sea and remained there throughout the conflict.

Bailey served as a cook on board HMS *Chester*, a light cruiser. The ship had a crew of 450 men, and was in the thick of the fighting at the Battle of Jutland in the North Sea (see page 14). At one point, Bailey and his shipmates were surrounded by four German light cruisers. They were hit by 17 150mm shells and suffered heavy losses, with 29 killed and 49 wounded. During fighting, cooks were assigned to ammunition supply, damage control, or casualty clearance. All of these roles involved considerable danger, but Bailey survived the battle unwounded.

Bailey and his wife Lilian had three children. Their sons James and Frank both became sailors, and their daughter, also named Lilian, became a Leading Aircraftwoman in the Women's Auxiliary Air Force.

Bailey continued to serve in the Merchant Navy until 1927, when he died aged 43. His grandson Geoffrey, although they never met, also followed in his footsteps to serve on HMS *Osprey*.

Francis Pegahmagabow was born on the Parry Island Reserve in Ontario, Canada, and enlisted with the 23rd Regiment (Northern Pioneers) in August 1914. He became one of the original members of the 1st Canadian Infantry Battalion which landed in France in February 1915.

Francis gained the nickname 'Peggy' and developed a reputation as an outstanding sniper and superior scout during the Second Battle of Ypres. He captured a large number of German prisoners at the Battle of Mount Sorrel in June 1916, for which he was awarded the Military medal.

At the Battle of Passchendaele, Francis was a runner whose job was to deliver **messages from the front of the battle informing the command at the rear about the location of the Canadian soldiers so that artillery bombardments might be successfully aimed at the German forces and not at the friendly ones. He was awarded a bar to his Military Medal in November 1917 for his bravery and excellent work during the Battle of Passchendaele. Francis was awarded a second bar for actions during the Battle of Amiens in August 1918.**

Francis was one of the few Canadian soldiers who enlisted in 1914 and fought to the end of the war; he was also one of Canada's most decorated Aboriginal soldiers in the First World War.

GERMAN WAR GRAVES COMMISSION

(VOLKSBUND DEUTSCHE KRIEGSGRÄBERFÜRSORGE)

HISTORY OF THE VOLKSBUND

The charitable organisation Volksbund Deutsche Kriegsgräberfürsorge was founded on 16 December 1919, in an emergency situation. During this post-war period, the German government was still young and was both politically and economically unable to look after the graves of those killed in the First World War, or care for their relatives. This task was undertaken by the Volksbund, which was founded following a citizens' initiative supported by the general population. Even now, two thirds of the Volksbund's funds come from sponsors and donors.

By the 1930s, the Volksbund had established numerous war graves. However, mourning those killed in the war was becoming increasingly appropriated by nationalism. In 1933, the leadership of the Volksbund became subject to the National Socialist regime. The establishing of military cemeteries during the Second World War was taken over by the grave service of the Wehrmacht, the Germany army.

In the year following the end of the Second World War, the Volksbund swiftly established over 400 war graves in Germany. In 1954, the federal government instructed the Volksbund to locate, secure, and maintain the graves of German soldiers abroad. After the political changes in Eastern Europe from 1989 onwards the Volksbund could start work there, too. **Today, the Volksbund looks after a total of 832 war grave cemeteries in 46 countries, where around 2.7 million victims of war are buried**.

GERMAN CULTURE OF REMEMBRANCE

The German War Graves Commission has always followed the principle of burying war victims where they fell. At the same time, the Volksbund tries to align these war graves for the most part with the sepulchral culture of the relevant country and local landscape. In some Eastern European countries, the Volksbund decided to use the group cemetery model due to the high numbers of victims. In such cases, groups of symbolic crosses are arranged in large fields, with the names of those buried there written on large monuments and in books of names laid out there.

Volunteer taking care of a monument documenting the buried soldiers at Stare Czarnowo war grave cemetery.

VOLKSBUND
Gemeinsam für den Frieden.

COLLECTIVE COMMEMORATION – DIFFERENTIATED REMEMBRANCE

We are working to establish remembrance in dialogue form. We wish to discover and understand the different historical experiences and remembrance cultures of our European neighbours, find common ground, and respect each other's differences. For these purposes, the Volksbund is working internationally with other participants in remembrance culture, collectively remembering victims of war. We see this international work as a contribution towards future peace and integration throughout Europe and the world.

A part of this is the critical reappraisal of German war crimes and human rights violations that took place during the Second World War and the Holocaust. The Volksbund looks after the graves of various groups of war dead: fallen soldiers, killed civilians, victims of the Holocaust, resistance fighters, but also war criminals. Dealing with these various groups of victims and perpetrators requires an exact contextualisation of the historical background, and a differentiated remembrance of an ambivalent history. This means that remembrance monuments are presented alongside various biographies and their historical contexts to share illustrative stories of war violence and persecution, as well as moral courage and humanity.

THE PEACE WORK OF THE VOLKSBUND: CURRENT PROJECTS

By maintaining cemeteries, the Volksbund ensures that victims of war continue to be remembered. It also performs an educational role, coming from the realisation that war graves are increasingly becoming places of both collective remembrance and of personal grief. More and more, they are developing into authentic historical places of learning for future generations. For this reason, their history needs to be presented and conveyed accordingly.

The Volksbund is supporting this change in meaning for war graves with political and historical work in its four youth exchange and education centres in Germany, the Netherlands, France, and Belgium. Every year, teenagers and young adults from all over the world meet up

Reburial at Stare Czarnowo war grave cemetery in Poland in 2018 with a group of symbolic crosses.

in dozens of international working projects throughout Europe. Information, permanent exhibitions, digital cemetery tours and a variety of other academic and extra-curricular educational projects turn cemeteries into places of learning and exchange, and bring the Volksbund's motto to life: 'Reconciliation above graves – work for peace'.

GERMAN STORIES

JOHANN KINAU (GORCH FOCK)

Died: 31.05.1916
Buried: Stensholmen War Cemetery, Sweden

In 1916, the German deep-sea fleet encountered the British Grand Fleet off the west coast of Denmark in the Battle of Jutland. Over 8,000 sailors from both sides lost their lives, including the writer Johann Kinau, better known by his pseudonym Gorch Fock.

Johann Kinau was born on 22 August 1880 on the island of Finkenwerder in the Elbe, near Hamburg. He was the eldest son of a fisherman. In 1907, Kinau took up the position of bookkeeper with the Hamburg-Amerika-Linie, and published his first poems in the Low German language. In some of his more well-known stories he described the austerity-filled lives of the Finkenwerder fishermen in an idealised style.

When the First World War broke out, Kinau served in the infantry, initially on the Eastern Front, after which he successfully applied for a transfer to the Navy in 1915. In the Battle of Jutland, Kinau lost his life when the small cruiser *Wiesbaden* sank. His body was later washed ashore onto the Swedish coast, and was buried along with other fallen German and British soldiers on the small island of Stensholmen.

To this day, Johann Kinau is remembered as one of the most distinguished German-language writers. Built in 1956, one of the German Navy's sail training ships, the three-mast barque *Gorch Fock*, was named after him.

COUNTESS KATHARINA VON DER SCHULENBURG

Died: 02.09.1914 or 09.09.1914
Buried: Vladslo German War Cemetery, Belgium

Countess Katharina von der Schulenburg was deaconess at the Saint Elisabeth Hospital in Berlin, and served as a senior nurse in the voluntary medical service, like many noblewomen during the First World War. Out of a total of 213,000 staff members of the medical service, at least 23,000 were nurses, assistant nurses, and helpers. These women participated voluntarily – they were paid very little, or not at all.

More than a third of the women worked near to the front line, where their lives were endangered. Shelters, train stations and vehicles transporting troops often came under fire from artillery or planes. In 1918, many medical staff members fell victim to the Spanish flu. There is a total of 18 women buried at the war grave in Vladslo, Belgium. Most of them worked as medical staff.

There are various accounts of Schulenburg's death: according to the German list of casualties, she died on 2nd September 1914 in the Belgian city of Tienen (Tirlemont) following a period of sickness. However, it is more probable that she lost her life there on 9th September 1914 when the train station came under fire from Belgian artillery. In her family chronicle, on the other hand, it is written that Schulenberg was murdered on 2nd September 1914 by Belgian partisans. There is no evidence for this.

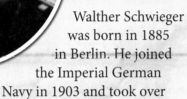

WALTHER SCHWIEGER

Lost: after 05.09.1917 in the North Sea

Walther Schwieger was born in 1885 in Berlin. He joined the Imperial German Navy in 1903 and took over command of the submarine U-20 in 1914. The initial battle victories of this new weapon of war became a myth among the public and led to an overestimation of its strategic utility. In February of 1915, the German Navy transitioned to a targeted commercial war with submarines. From then on, all commercial ships met within the restricted areas were attacked without warning.

On May 7, 1915, U-20 sank the British passenger steamer *Lusitania*, killing 1198 people, including 120 American citizens.

Schwieger had erroneously identified the ship as an armed auxiliary cruiser. From the German side, it was suspected that the detonation of munitions illegally carried on board contributed to the rapid sinking of the ship. Today, however, it is assumed that a carbon dust explosion was the cause.

To this day, it is disputed whether the sinking of the *Lusitania* was a war crime. However, the outrage over the death of so many civilians led to strong protests, including on the part of the neutral US government, and the unrestricted submarine war was temporarily suspended as a result.

Regardless, the submarine war had little influence on the course of the war, despite the many losses. Schwieger and his crew were lost after departing Helgoland for a tour in 1917.

BROTHERS: HERMANN AND HEINRICH BETKE

Died: 03.11.1914 and 11.11.1914
Buried: Menen German War Cemetery, Belgium

Heinrich Betke was born in 1878, and his brother Hermann was born two years later. They grew up on their father's farm near the city of Detmold/ Westphalia. The two brothers spent their military service as *'Spielleute'* (military musicians) in the 55th Infantry Regiment *'Graf Bülow von Dennewitz'* in Detmold.

After their time in the army, Heinrich and Hermann found work in the then bustling brick-making industry in Varel/Lower Saxony. Heinrich married his wife Marie in 1910. Their son Heinrich was born in 1913. Hermann married his wife

Antonie in 1905. They had two children together (Hernanda, born in 1906, and Gustav, born in 1907).

At the beginning of the First World War, Hermann and Heinrich Betke were drafted into the 1st Company of the 4th Reserve Ersatz Regiment. The regiment fought in the First Battle of Ypres against British troops. From 26th October to 13th November 1914, the regiment participated in the unsuccessful attempt of the German Army to take over the strategically important crossroads near Broodseinde, east of Ypres. During the heavy fighting, the regiment lost a total of 625 soldiers. Two of them were Heinrich and Hermann Betke. They fell on 3rd and 11th November.

SPORTS AT WAR

When war broke out, professional and amateur sports were an important part of life. This continued throughout the conflict, as people at home and on the front line found ways to use their sporting talents to support the war effort and keep up morale.

RUGBY

Rugby teams often joined up together and, sadly, quite often died together, too. Twenty-seven England Rugby Internationals died in the First World War, and so did huge numbers of club-and school-level players. More Scottish rugby internationals were killed than from any other nation, and the captain of the first All Blacks side to tour Britain, the 'Invincibles' of 1905, was killed in Flanders in 1917. **Men who enlisted took their love of rugby to the Front with them, and many tournaments were played including against French army sides.** In the Somme Cup in 1917, the 'Trench All Blacks', representing New Zealand, were victorious. This was actually their second victory! New Zealand also won a tournament against Australia at Gallipoli in 1915, played on a sandy beach at low tide. The New Zealanders defeated the Australians 13 tries to nil – even though there were no goals kicked as they didn't have any goalposts! The following day, the two teams fought alongside each other against the Ottoman Empire (see page 48).

"This is not the time to play Games" (Lord Roberts)

RUGBY · UNION · FOOTBALLERS
are
DOING · THEIR · DUTY
over 90% have enlisted

"Every player who represented England in Rugby international matches last year has joined the colours."—Extract from The Times, November 30, 1914.

BRITISH ATHLETES!
Will you follow this
GLORIOUS EXAMPLE ?

A poster encouraging rugby lovers to enlist.

CRICKET

When war broke out, hundreds of amateurs playing county cricket with commissions in the Territorial Army joined their regiments, and many professional cricketers enlisted as volunteers. The buildings at Lord's, Old Trafford, Trent Bridge and the county grounds of Derbyshire and Leicestershire were used as accommodation for army units and military hospitals, and many cricket clubs allowed their grounds to be farmed to help the war effort.

British troops on the Western Front organised matches between regiments, or between officers and sergeants, and often charity matches took place on the Home Front to raise money for the war effort. In fact the game was even used as a decoy! **While ANZAC troops were evacuating from Gallipoli (see page 56), the Australians staged a huge cricket match to distract the Turkish troops.** They played a match in full view of the Turks and with shells flying overhead, to make it seem like things were normal while thousands of men were being secretly evacuated from the beach by night!

Colin Blythe, Kent and England left-arm spin bowler and one of the greatest cricketers of the time. Colin enlisted in August 1914 and died aged 38 on 8th November 1917. He is commemorated at Oxford Road Cemetery, Belgium.

DID YOU KNOW...?

EIGHTEEN THOUSAND HAY-NETS FOR WAR HORSES WERE MADE AT LORD'S CRICKET GROUND!

FOOTBALL

Football has long been an important part of British culture, and was used to keep up morale at the Front. **At Christmas 1914, there was a truce, and soldiers set aside their weapons. It was rumoured that a game of football took place between British and German troops in No Man's Land.** Whether or not this match against the Germans really occurred, games of football on the front line were a common occurrence.

At home, women's football became a huge sport, with crowds of 10,000 turning out to matches to raise money for war charities. In 1918, the Munitionettes Cup was held, with 30 teams competing in front of a 20,000-strong crowd and Blyth Spartans Ladies FC becoming champions!

Women munitions workers' football team from the AEC Munitions Factory at Beckton, London.

WALTER TULL (1888-1918)

Walter Tull was born in Folkestone in 1888. His father had arrived from Barbados in 1876, and his mother was from Kent. Both of Walter's parents died when he was still a child.

Walter was a keen footballer, and in 1908 his talents were discovered by a scout from Tottenham Hotspur, and he played for the London team until 1910, when he was transferred to Northampton Town.

When war was declared in 1914, Walter gave up his football career to join the 17th (1st Football) Battalion of the Middlesex Regiment.

Walter was promoted three times during his training. Whilst fighting on the Western Front in 1915, he was sent home with post-traumatic disorder, but returned to fight in the Battle of the Somme in 1916 (see page 12). Walter's superiors were impressed by his courage and abilities and

recommended him as an officer. On 25th March 1918 he was killed in action during the First Battle of Bapaume. His body was never recovered. Even though black soldiers were officially barred from becoming officers, Walter was commissioned as a Second Lieutenant.

On 25th March 1918, Lieutenant Tull was killed by machine gun fire during an attempt to breach German lines on the Western Front. Walter's body was never found and he is one of the thousands of soldiers from the war who have no known grave.

THE WAR IN THE SKIES

The development of aircraft was motivated by the demands of modern warfare. At first, aircraft were used for reconnaissance missions, in which the pilot or his observer would feed information back about the movements of German troops; help direct artillery strikes; or take photographs showing enemy positions and gun batteries. As time went on, aircraft increasingly became weapons, as more powerful engines allowed them to be fitted with guns and bombs.

AIRSHIPS

At the beginning of the First World War, Germany had 10 Zeppelins and three smaller airships. However, a problem with them quickly became apparent: they were extremely explosive! The German Army stopped airship operations as losses became too frequent early in the war, but meanwhile the German Navy began night bombing offensives, the first aerial strategic bombardment campaign in history.

Airships were large targets, so it was common for them to be shot down, and it is for this reason **the First World War was the last time airships were used as combat aircraft**. Throughout the war they were used mainly for anti-submarine patrols, convoy escort and protection, and coastal reconnaissance.

Lieutenant Warneford's Great Exploit: the first Zeppelin to be brought down by Allied aircraft, 7th June 1915; oil on canvas by Frederick Gordon Crosby.

OBSERVATION AIRCRAFT

Balloons: Observation balloons were particularly useful along the Western Front. Above the trenches and anchored to the ground, the balloons were able to see what was beyond the enemy's front line, including being able to locate their artillery. Often an observer would be alone in the balloon, collecting information about the enemy side and passing it to the ground by telephone. This was a dangerous job, as they were a huge, stationary target. Some men took pride in shooting down these balloons, getting reputations as 'balloon busters': for example, Willy Coppens brought down 35 balloons, the highest single total of the war.

Reconnaissance aircraft: Due to their small engines, these aeroplanes could often only support a pilot and occasionally an observer. At the Battle of the Marne, information the British and French armies received from aircraft made possible the successful counter-attack on the Germans, who were forced to retreat. Aircraft continued to develop throughout the war, with more powerful engines enabling the planes to fly higher and thereby avoid interception! For example, in 1917 the Germans created a plane that could operate as high as 24,000 feet!

FIGHTER PLANES

Observation planes presented a huge problem. Neither side wanted the other to know where their artillery was so they could keep it safe from shelling! In the early years, pilots and observers would fire at enemy planes with pistols, rifles and shotguns. But this was fairly unsuccessful.

In 1913, fighter planes began to be fitted with machines guns, which were often fired by an observer who would have sat ahead of the pilot. Aerial warfare became deadlier in July 1915 when Dutch aircraft designer **Anton Fokker developed a timing mechanism that synchronised the machine gun with the propeller, allowing bullets to fly between the turning blades**.

Both sides developed fighter aircraft intended to shoot down the enemy's planes, such as the German Fokkers and the British Sopwith Camels. They also developed aircraft capable of carrying bombs which could be dropped on enemy targets.

Closing Up by Horace Davis (1881–1963). Davis was a landscape painter who served in the RAF. He instituted aerial manoeuvre diagrams to train pilots, and was commissioned by the Imperial War Museum to paint two of these manoeuvres.

My plane had an open cockpit, so it was extremely cold! I had to wear warm clothing, like my sheepskin jacket.

THE BLOW-BOMB.
AN ENGINE FOR BLOWING OUT THE FUSES OF ZEPPELIN BOMBS.

A cartoon by William Heath Robinson, *The Blow-Bomb*.

THE WAR IN THE SKIES

Britain had two forces in the air – The Royal Flying Corps (RFC), run by the Army, and the Royal Navy Air Service (RNAS), created by the Navy. In April 1918, the two air forces were combined into one, the Royal Air Force (RAF).

ROYAL FLYING CORPS

The Royal Flying Corps was created in 1912 and played an important role in the First World War. The RFC were busy observing the enemy from the start of the War, and after the beginning of trench warfare began taking the first of millions of aerial photographs of enemy positions.

In 1916, South Asian and British soldiers were fighting in Mesopotamia (modern Iraq) and trying to lift the Siege of Kut (see page 51). This was unsuccessful, and caused over 23,000 deaths. Lack of food was the most serious problem for those trapped in the city, who suffered scurvy and other diseases. **Food and medicine drops by the Royal Flying Corps were arranged, possibly for the first time in history**. But the British planes had to contend with German and Turkish planes defending the siege. Between 15th and 29th April, 19,000 pounds of supplies were dropped in 140 flights.

Sadly, despite all their efforts, the situation was still desperate and the Allies had to surrender on 29th April 1916.

Bags of grain being dropped over Kut by a British Maurice Farman biplane opposed by a German Fokker.

ROYAL NAVY AIR SERVICE (RNAS)

The Navy's air force was active at sea and on land from the outset of the war. **At sea, the RNAS made great strides operating seaplanes with floats to land on the water**. Naval versions of land planes, which could not land on water, could fly back to an airfield or 'ditch' in the sea next to a rescue ship. Over land, the Navy's air force was used against the Zeppelins, German airships.

By the time the Royal Air Force (RAF) was created in April 1918, the RNAS had already undertaken a strategic bombing campaign against munitions factories and steelworks. Later, the RAF also attacked German industry and communications and by the end of the war it was using twin-engined Handley Page bombers capable of carrying nearly a ton of bombs.

CREATION OF THE RAF

A problem with having two air services (RFC and RNAS) was the constant competition between them for engines and aircraft. When the Germans bombed London in 1917, the British government decided something needed to be done and an idea of uniting the two was discussed. Some felt this would be impossible. Prime Minister David Lloyd George turned to General Jan Smuts to solve these problems, and fast.

Smuts suggested an Air Ministry and Air Staff to combine the RFC and the RNAS into a new Air Service that would be independent of the Army and the Navy. However, many believed unifying would be far too difficult during the war, and others believed that the air services should be supporting land operations and did not have the experience to be independent.

The worries were not enough to dissuade Smuts, and the Royal Air force (RAF) was born in April 1918.

WOMEN'S ROYAL AIR FORCE (WRAF)

The Women's Royal Naval Service (WRNS) and the Women's Army Auxiliary Corps (WAAC, see page 20) worked on different air stations which belonged to the RFC and RNAS. When they merged to create the RAF, it seemed necessary to make a new women's force, and so the WRAF was formed on 1st April 1918. In total, 32,000 women joined the WRAF.

These women were given the choice to transfer, and over 9,000 did. Initially, this growing unit worked only in Britain, but as the war went on they were needed elsewhere, moving to France and Germany in 1919.

By 1920, there were over 50 trades the WRAF offered, from pigeon-keeping to driving. Although this unit was a vital asset to the RAF, it was still only a wartime force, and in 1920 it was disbanded.

WRAFs Drilling At Andover Aerodrome by Fairlie Harmar, Viscountess Harberton (1876–1945). A group of Women's Royal Air Force personnel engaged in military drill on the tarmac outside an aircraft hangar. Behind them are two biplanes standing on the tarmac, with two other planes in the sky above.

IRISH WAR POETS

There is no echo in the works of Tom Kettle and Francis Ledwidge of Owen's 'doomed youth' or of Sassoon's dismissal of the officer class as 'incompetent swine'. Their writings contain more echoes of Rupert Brooke's 'foreign field that is forever' – Ireland. As Irish nationalists, they persisted to the end in their belief in the essential nobility of the task in which they were engaged. They adhered to the view of Irish parliamentary leader, John Redmond, for whom the war was a struggle 'in defence of rights and freedom and religion'. The stories of Kettle and Ledwidge provide an intriguing insight into Irish involvement in the First World War. Their poetic responses to the war differed from those of their English literary counterparts.

FRANCIS LEDWIDGE (1887-1917)

Francis Ledwidge

Francis Ledwidge decided to enlist in the Royal Inniskilling Fusiliers and his first introduction to the war was at Gallipoli. He wrote no poetry during the eight weeks he spent on the campaign, but was lucky enough to be included among the 118,000 men who were evacuated from the peninsula.

While recovering from an inflamed back in Manchester in 1916, Francis received news of the Easter Rising in Dublin and the executions of nationalist leaders that followed it, including his good friend and fellow poet Thomas MacDonagh. He became completely disillusioned and declared: 'If someone was to tell me now that the Germans were coming over our back wall, I wouldn't lift a finger to stop them. They should come'.

In July 1917, having survived the Battle of Arras, Francis's unit was ordered north to Belgium in preparation for the Battle of Passchendaele. On 31st July, the 1st Battalion of the Royal Inniskilling Fusiliers, of which Francis was a member, were repairing the road to Pilkem near the village of Boezinghe, northwest of Ypres. In the afternoon of that day, a shell exploded beside them, killing one officer and five enlisted men, among them Francis.

DID YOU KNOW...?

206,000 IRISHMEN FOUGHT IN BRITISH UNIFORM, AND SOME 49,000 LOST THEIR LIVES.

A Soldier's Grave
Francis Ledwidge

Then in the lull of midnight, gentle arms
Lifted him slowly down the slopes of death,
Lest he should hear again the mad alarms
Of battle, dying moans, and painful breath.

And where the earth was soft for flowers we made
A grave for him that he might better rest.
So, Spring shall come and leave it sweet arrayed,
And there the lark shall turn her dewy nest.

TOM KETTLE (1880-1916)

In 1913, Tom Kettle joined the Irish Volunteers, a paramilitary group set up in opposition to the Ulster Volunteers as a part of the struggle for Irish Home Rule. **Visiting Belgium in the summer of 1914, on a mission to purchase arms for the Irish Volunteers, Tom witnessed at first hand the German invasion of that country. He, like many Irish nationalists, sympathised deeply with the plight of Belgium.** From the start, he saw the war as a struggle for civilised European values against the threat posed by Imperial Germany and became convinced that Britain's support of Belgium would be a precursor to subsequent support for Irish Home Rule – already committed to by the British government in London, albeit delayed in its implementation by the outbreak of war.

Tom returned to Ireland and became a recruiting officer. Often criticised by other nationalists for his recruiting activities, he once stated that, if forced to choose, he cared for liberty more than he cared for Ireland.

Tom requested that he be sent to fight in France in the Battle of the Somme and was killed during an attack on Givenchy on 9th September 1916.

To My Daughter Betty, The Gift of God
Tom Kettle

In wiser days, my darling rosebud, blown
To beauty proud as was your mother's prime,
In that desired, delayed, incredible time,
You'll ask why I abandoned you, my own,
And the dear heart that was your baby throne,
To dice with death. And oh! they'll give you rhyme
And reason: some will call the thing sublime,
And some decry it in a knowing tone.
So here, while the mad guns curse overhead,
And tired men sigh with mud for couch and floor,
Know that we fools, now with the foolish dead,
Died not for flag, nor King, nor Emperor,
But for a dream, born in a herdsman's shed,
And for the secret Scripture of the poor.

DID YOU KNOW...?

TOM KETTLE WROTE 'TO MY DAUGHTER BETTY, THE GIFT OF GOD' JUST DAYS BEFORE HIS DEATH – IN THIS POEM HE TRIES TO EXPLAIN TO HIS DAUGHTER WHY HE HAD SACRIFICED HIS LIFE.

JEWISH COMMUNITY

In 1914, the Jewish population of Britain was approximately 250,000–300,000, with a further estimated 40,000 resident in Australia, Canada and New Zealand. Jews accounted for less than 1% of the population in each country, but on the outbreak of the First World War they joined up in high numbers. 40,000 Jews are known to have served in the British armed forces, although the figure is likely to be 50,000–55,000, since many hid their religion to avoid anti-Semitism.

BRITISH JEWS DURING THE FIRST WORLD WAR

Jews served in many regiments of the British Army, as well as in the Royal Navy, the Royal Flying Corps and the newly formed Royal Air Force. Jewish women became nurses, Voluntary Aid Detachment members (VADs) and Red Cross workers. They were employed in many areas on the Home Front, including in munitions factories and Government offices. **Florence Oppenheimer, a Queen Alexandria Imperial Military Nursing Service nurse, served in the Middle East. After the war, she became a famous cookery writer under her married name, Florence Greenberg**.

DAVID BOMBERG (1890–1957)

David Bomberg was part of the Jewish Whitechapel Group alongside fellow artist Mark Gertler and fellow artist and poet Isaac Rosenberg (see page 107).

In 1914, the Germans exploded mines under British positions at Festubert, Belgium, in an attempt to break the stalemate of trench warfare. In response, the British recruited professional miners to dig tunnels at the Western Front to detonate mines beneath German trenches. The launch of the Messines offensive (see page 41) in June 1917 witnessed 19 mines exploding, one of which was the largest mine of the war. In 1918, having served with the Royal Engineers, David was commissioned by the Canadian government to paint this operation.

David was influenced by Cubism and Futurism, and was a major figure in the London avant-garde. David has included himself in the foreground carrying a heavy beam; it is thought that he is showing his feeling of being burdened by this task.

Sappers at Work: Canadian Tunnelling Company by David Bomberg.

DID YOU KNOW...?

THERE WERE NO RESTRICTIONS ON JEWS JOINING THE BRITISH MILITARY OR BECOMING COMMISSIONED OFFICERS PRIOR TO THE FIRST WORLD WAR, UNLIKE IN OTHER EUROPEAN COUNTRIES.

BRITISH JEWRY BOOK OF HONOUR

In 1922, the *British Jewry Book of Honour* was published in London to permanently record and honour the contribution made by the Jews who served in the British and colonial forces during the war. The book was edited by the Reverend Michael Adler, who was the first Jewish chaplain to serve in HM Forces. It lists casualties, military honours, the names of those who served, Jewish units, and where possible, other Jewish institutions and agencies that supported the Home Front and the wider war effort. The book also contains letters of support and acknowledgment from distinguished men of the day, both Jewish and non-Jewish.

THE ZION MULE CORPS AND THE ROYAL FUSILIERS

Some Jewish men in Britain did not have British or Empire citizenship, and were consequently unable to join the regular armed services. In Palestine, Jews from Russia, Turkey and elsewhere lobbied the British government to be allowed to join up. These men were eventually formed into the Zion Mule Corps and saw service in Gallipoli, where they received much praise from the British authorities. Once the Dardanelles campaign ended, the Corps was disbanded. Many of its members campaigned for a new version of the Corps, and so **a new Jewish regiment was formed in 1917, which became the 38th, 39th, 40th and 42nd Battalions of the Royal Fusiliers**.

These Battalions included Jews from Britain, Russia, other Empire and Allied nations and the USA. In 1919, those still serving were given a regimental cap badge depicting a Menorah (a Jewish candelabra). The Battalions were disbanded between 1919 and 1921.

FRANK ALEXANDER DE PASS (1887– 1914)

Frank Alexander De Pass.

De Pass was a Londoner who joined the army as an officer in 1906. In 1914, he was serving as a lieutenant with a British regiment in India when he was sent to France. **On 24th November 1914, De Pass destroyed an enemy trench and rescued an injured fellow soldier during intense fighting**. He was awarded the Victoria Cross, but died before the news could reach him; he was killed on 25th November 1914.

ART & ARTISTS

One of the unexpected benefits of the First World War was the large amount of funding suddenly made available to artists by the British government. Public demand for information was high, and the government responded by commissioning hundreds of artists – many of them fighting on the front lines – to depict the war as they saw it. The results were diverse and numerous.

Even though the British propaganda department was behind the commissionings, and many artists saw it as their duty to respond, the paintings and sculptures did not shrink from depicting the reality of war.

JOHN SINGER SARGENT

Gassed, 1919

John Singer Sargent was born in Florence to American parents and began training in Paris in 1874 with the portraitist Carolus-Duran. John was a portrait painter and was also known for his stunning, jarring landscapes.

In 1918, the British Government commissioned him to go to the front line of the First World War to paint a commemorative work of their troops in action. The result, **Gassed, depicts the aftermath of a mustard gas attack on the Western Front in August 1918 as witnessed by the artist.** Mustard gas was an indiscriminate weapon that caused widespread injury and burns, as well as affecting the eyes.

John was commissioned by the British Government to contribute the central painting for a Hall of Remembrance for the First World War. He was given the theme of 'Anglo-American cooperation', but was unable to find suitable subject matter and chose this scene instead.

MUIRHEAD BONE

Château near Brie on the Somme, 1918

Muirhead Bone was apprenticed to an architect, but took evening classes at the Glasgow School of Art, where he studied architecture and painting. **He settled in London in 1901 and was the first person to be appointed an Official War Artist after lobbying hard for the scheme.**

Muirhead served as a war artist with the Allied forces on the Western Front and also with the Royal Navy for a time. He arrived in France during the Battle of the Somme in 1916 and returned in 1917, when he took particular interest in depicting architectural ruins.

The nascent Vorticist movement turned its already surreal and brutal style to showing the horrors of the Western Front, with dark and disturbing results. It may not have been the British propaganda machine's top priority, but the honest, avant-garde nature of the works helped to cast Britain as a leader in postwar liberal culture.

As with the poets, the variety of the painters' work reflects conflicted feelings towards the war. Anna Airy depicts the step forward that the war was for women, while Percy Wyndham Lewis reminds us of the sacrifices.

PERCY WYNDHAM LEWIS

A Battery Shelled, 1919

Percy Wyndham Lewis came to England from Canada as a child and studied at the Slade School of Fine Art in London from 1898 to 1901. In the years leading up to the First World War, Percy emerged as one of the chief figures in the British avant-garde. **He was a founding member of the Vorticists – Vorticism was an artistic movement that used aggressive, angular lines to emphasise the upheaval brought about by the Machine Age**. The style draws on elements of Cubism and Futurism.

Lewis served as a battery officer in the Royal Garrison Artillery on the Western Front from 1915 to 1917, and was an Official War Artist from 1917 to 1918. His depiction here of counter-battery fire experienced by the artillerymen was therefore drawn from personal experience on the Western Front.

ANNA AIRY

Women Working in a Gas Retort House: South Metropolitan Gas Company, London, 1918

Anna Airy trained at the Slade with William Orpen and Augustus John, and was one of the first women war artists employed by the Imperial War Museum in 1918. Although a well-respected female artist of her generation, the committee imposed strict terms on her contract of employment, which included their right to refuse a work without payment. She was commissioned to produce a series of works depicting typical scenes in munitions production and other aspects of heavy industry where women had taken over from men. **Anna painted her canvases on site, in awkward and at times dangerous conditions**.

Here women work on the gas retort process, where gas was produced from coal by burning it in the absence of air. It must have been a difficult place to work, not only for the women in the painting, but also for the painter herself.

SPIES

In a book written in the fifth century BCE, a famous Chinese military leader, Sun Tzu, devoted a whole chapter to 'The Use of Spies'. He reached the conclusion that 'what enables the wise sovereign and the good general to strike and conquer, and achieve things beyond the reach of ordinary men, is foreknowledge'. Between 1914 and 1918, both sides did their utmost to recruit, train and use spies to gather that 'foreknowledge'. Although men were sent close to the battle fronts, women worked behind the lines on both sides. Spies' watchful eyes and listening ears provided both sides with intelligence about what was going on behind the scenes.

ELISABETH SCHRAGMÜLLER AKA FRAULEIN DOKTOR

(1887–1940)

Elisabeth Schragmüller

Elisabeth Schragmüller was the first German woman to become a doctor, not of medicine but of Political Economy. However, she is remembered best for being a spymaster during the war.

Code-named Fraulein Doktor, in August 1914, Elisabeth was desperate to 'do her bit' for Germany's war effort. At first, Germany wasn't convinced Elisabeth could be useful, but eventually the military authorities sent her to Antwerp in German-occupied Belgium. **Elisabeth was tasked with the important job of recruiting and training spies to be sent throughout France**. Elisabeth organised a spy school to teach recruits many skills as well as how to develop secret codes, create invisible ink and miniature handwriting. Messages were hidden in accessories such as umbrellas, in shoe heels, hollowed-out vegetables, rolled into tiny packages or enclosed in small pieces of inflammable materials stuffed inside a cigar or cigarette. If someone dangerous approached, they just lit up and puffed away!

Elisabeth didn't care if her spies were men or women; all that mattered was their ability. She found excellent spies in unlikely places. **One of her best operatives was a florist who couldn't read or write, but who was brilliant at remembering what he had seen; he had a 'photographic memory'**. It has been estimated that Elisabeth sent over 100 female agents into France (20 were caught) and at least four times as many men.

DID YOU KNOW...?

SOME 'STUDENTS' COULD WRITE UP TO 1,600 WORDS ON A POSTAGE STAMP.

Marthe Cnockaert in around 1920.

MARTHE CNOCKAERT
(1892–1966)

During the summer of 1914, Martha Cnockaert was training to be a doctor, and on the outbreak of war she was conscripted to work as a nurse at a German Military Hospital near her home in Roulers, Belgium.

A British spymaster approached Martha to be a spy, to which she agreed out of a sense of loyalty to Belgium. She was told to gather information about troop movements around Roulers station, an important railhead for the Germans. In spring 1915, thanks to her information, the Allies bombed the station.

Martha describes how she had 'wandered along an endless street of smoking ruins where the way was strewn with mangled corpses whose glassy eyeballs watched me accusingly'.

On 22nd April 1915, both German and Allied casualties of the first gas attack flooded into her hospital. **Martha's dedication to her patients earned her the German Iron Cross, which was presented to her by King William II, the last royal ruler of Württemberg.**

The Germans then asked Martha to spy for them, but she refused. She fell into a trap they set. In November 1916, she was arrested. The court found her guilty, and she was sentenced to death. Roulers Military Hospital's Chief Doctor spoke out in her defence. Her sentence was changed to life imprisonment.

After the war, Martha was mentioned in British General Sir Douglas Haig's Dispatches. The French and the Belgian Légions d'honneur followed, making her the only person to have been decorated by four of the main combatants of the Great War.

Roulers after the bombardment.

Think about what sort of people would be useful in the 'spy business'.

SPIES

LOUISE DE BETTIGNIES

(1880-1918)

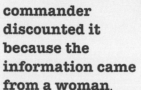

The 'Joan of Arc of the North'

Born in Lille, France, Louise de Bettignies was exceptionally clever and spoke five languages fluently, including English. When the Germans captured Lille in October 1914, the British recruited her to spy for them in Occupied France. At an English spy school she learnt how to create miniature maps, to write in invisible ink on tissue paper, to engrave minute letters on spectacle frames, and to conceal messages in shoe heels, umbrella handles, hems of skirts and hollowed-out vegetables.

She used her map-drawing skills to create a miniature map of the German lines showing 2,000 gun positions. The Germans called the 40 kilometres (25 miles) where her networks operated the 'cursed' front; this was where they seemed to suffer the greatest number of unexpected attacks and aerial bombardments.

Sadly, her information was sometimes ignored. **When Louise reported that the Germans were preparing a massive attack on Verdun in early 1916, the French commander discounted it because the information came from a woman**. The Battle of Verdun resulted in 262,308 French and German dead or missing.

Louise was arrested in autumn 1915 and went to trial the following March. The Germans sentenced her to life imprisonment with hard labour. During the winter of 1917, Louise developed pleurisy and died on 27th September 1918, 45 days before the Armistice.

She had been mentioned in Marshal Joffre's dispatches in April 1916, and was awarded the French Légion d'honneur, the Croix de guerre 1914–18 with palm, the British Military Medal and the OBE.

In November 1927, a monument to Louise de Bettignies and the 'heroic women' of the Occupied Territories was unveiled in her native city.

Monument to Louise in Lille from *La France reconnaissante* (a Grateful France).

Memorial to Louise at Notre Dame de Lorette.

Gabrielle Petit

Gabrielle Petit, a 21-year-old shop assistant in Brussels, was furious when Germany occupied her city on 20th August 1914. She wanted to share her knowledge of the surrounding area and activities of the Germans with the British. In July 1915 she was invited by the British authorities to London's Spy School.

Back in Brussels, she soon created her own spy network. She crossed backwards and forwards between occupied France and Belgium carrying top secret information and she was always on the lookout for anything the Allies might find useful.

Gabrielle was arrested on 20th January 1916 and thrown into St Gilles Prison, Brussels. At every interrogation she stressed her loathing of the Germans. After a trial conducted in German, she spoke only French, and without knowing anyone influential to plead on her behalf, Gabrielle was sentenced to death by firing squad.

After the war, combatant nations sought to memorialise their glorious dead. In Belgium someone thought of the little Brussels shop assistant, Gabrielle, and decided that she would become Belgium's martyr. **In May 1919, her body was exhumed; at an elaborate funeral the Belgian queen awarded Gabrielle the Croix de l'Ordre de Léopold**. Gabrielle's statue still stands in Brussels' Place St Jean. Her effigy looks down proudly on passers-by and reminds them that, poor and young though she was, Gabrielle Petit had known both how to spy and how to die for her beloved Belgium.

The inscription reads: 'You will see that a Belgian woman knows how to die'.

Memorial to Gabrielle in the National Arboretum, unveiled 1st April 2016.

THE WAR AT SEA

Laws introduced in Germany in 1899 encouraged a naval arms race between Britain and Germany, with the German government hoping that a powerful German fleet would prevent Britain from intervening in a war in Europe. The naval arms race was largely between two Dreadnought (a type of battleship) programmes.

NAVAL TACTICS

Germany began the U-boat campaign at the very start of the war with an aim to sink merchant ships bringing vital supplies to Britain, which relied on imports from all over the world.

In 1915, Germany turned to 'unrestricted submarine warfare', where merchant ships were sunk without warning, regardless of nationality. This tactic swayed public opinion in the USA, which had previously remained neutral, against Germany (see page 38). **By 1917, Germany had more submarines carrying more torpedoes, and so, to reduce losses of merchant ships, the Royal Navy started using convoys.** As the convoys approached Britain, they would be met by naval escort vessels and aircraft to protect them from attack.

Blockades were a common tactic during the First World War. In the Mediterranean, the Royal Navy contributed to the blockade of both the Austro-Hungarian and the Ottoman empires. The longest of these blockades was the one on Germany (see page 32).

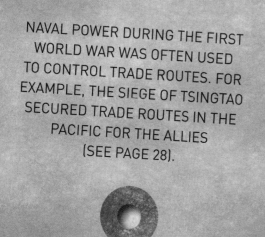

NAVAL POWER DURING THE FIRST WORLD WAR WAS OFTEN USED TO CONTROL TRADE ROUTES. FOR EXAMPLE, THE SIEGE OF TSINGTAO SECURED TRADE ROUTES IN THE PACIFIC FOR THE ALLIES (SEE PAGE 28).

U-boats were able to sink only one ship that was being escorted by an aircraft.

Years Ahead
Guy N Pocock (1880–1955)

Days to come, days to come
But who shall ask of the wandering foam,
The weaving weed, or the rocking swell,
The place of our sailor-dead to tell ?
From Jutland reefs to Scapa Flow
Tracks of the wary warships go,
But the deep sea-wastes lie green and dumb
All the days to come.

Years ahead, years ahead,
The sea shall honour our sailor-dead !
No mound of mouldering earth shall show
The fighting place of the men below,
But a swirl of seas that gather and spill;
And the wind's wild chanty whistling shrill
Shall cry 'Consider my sailor-dead!'
In the years ahead.

[Extract]

MERCHANT NAVY

Germany's 'unrestricted submarine warfare' meant that it was very dangerous to serve in the Merchant Navy. Merchant sailors were recruited from across the British Empire, including from Hong Kong, western African countries, Jamaica, Barbados and other British territories in the West Indies.

About 14,000 merchant sailors died during the First World War; 4,000 were killed during a three-month period in 1917. Some of the many who lost their lives are commemorated on the Commonwealth War Graves Commission's Tower Hill Memorial in London.

DARDANELLES

In February 1915, Britain tried to force the Ottoman Empire out of the war by taking Royal Navy warships through the narrow Dardanelles and attacking Constantinople. **On 18th March 1915, three ships were sunk and three more were badly damaged by Turkish mines prior to the Allied landing at Gallipoli** (see page 48).

When it was clear that the Allies could not win, it was the Navy's job to evacuate the Army, but its role in the Mediterranean did not end there. The Royal Navy supported Allied land operations in Egypt, Palestine and Macedonia, as well as keeping open the routes between Europe and Asia via the Suez Canal.

HMS Queen Elizabeth *Shelling Forts, Dardanelles. The attack on the Narrows, Gallipoli, 18th March, 1915* by Norman Wilkinson (1878–1971).

The German submarine U-21 sank HMS *Pathfinder* on 5th September 1914, the day before the Battle of the Marne (see page 13).

THE WAR AT SEA

THE NORTH SEA

In the winter of 1915–16, a massive naval battle in the North Sea was expected, but the German Navy was not strong enough to risk a meeting. Instead they opted for raid on the British coast. The German Navy hoped to gradually whittle down British superiority to the point where they could meet the British Royal Navy on equal terms. The British moved their Grand Fleet to the relative security of Scapa Flow, in the Orkney Islands, and so the North Sea became a maritime no man's land.

The Battle of Jutland to the British (Battle of Skaggerak to the Germans) began on 31st May 1916 and was the only time a massed fleet of huge battleships fought head-to-head. The long-awaited clash ended inconclusively, as both sides claimed victory. The British lost more ships, but after the battle the German fleet rarely ventured out of its harbours (see page 14).

The Second Division at Jutland by W L Wyllie (1851–1931).

ST GEORGE'S DAY RAID

On 23rd April 1918 (St George's Day), the British naval forces planned to block German access to the North Sea at Zeebrugge and Ostend in Belgium by launching an amphibious raid on the mole which provided shelter for U-boats in the harbour and protected access to their inland base. Three British ships were deliberately sunk in the harbour to block access. **The raid did not succeed in blocking the submarine canal, but it was hailed as a daring and courageous attack, raising public morale in Britain**.

The 63rd Royal Navy division fought in a number of land battles during the war, including Gallipoli, the Somme, Gayrell and Passchendaele. Over 10,000 of its men were killed fighting on the Western Front.

St George's Day 1918: Bridge of HMS Canterbury by Philip Connard (1875–1958). When the Great Naval Raid took place on Zeebrugge and Ostend, HMS *Canterbury* was on patrol work.

MINEFIELD ACROSS DOVER

In response to the German U-boat campaign, the Royal Navy set up the Dover Barrage. This operation started early in the war and involved laying a huge minefield between the coast of Belgium and Dover.

The intention was to deter the U-boats from accessing this area. The barrage was set up with nets to trap the enemy's ship, and a large minefield.

The minefield did not always prove successful.

The mines were not always reliable, and the netting was not always perfectly positioned, sometimes leaving gaps for the German U-boats to duck under.

HMS Firedrake *Signalling 'MN' (Stop Immediately) to German U-Boats, 20th November 1918* – a panoramic seascape sketch by Francis Dodd (1874–1949) of a warship with signal flags hoisted, four submarines and an airship above.

WOMEN'S ROYAL NAVAL SERVICE (WRNS)

The Women's Royal Naval Service (WRNS), sometimes known as 'the Wrens', was formed in 1917. The Wrens were cooks, stewards, despatch riders, sail-makers and worked in intelligence. Some women transferred from WRNS to WRAF when that was formed in 1918 (see page 77).

By the end of the war, there were 7,000 Wrens and, although the unit proved successful to the war effort, it was disbanded when the war was over.

THE GRAND SCUTTLE

On the morning of 21st November 1918, HMS *Cardiff*, a light cruiser, met the German High Seas Fleet. The German ships were led towards the British Grand Fleet and surrendered. They anchored at Scapa Flow and waited while negotiations took place at Versailles (see page 126).

After the Armistice, all surviving German U-boats and ships were surrendered under the terms of the Treaty of Versailles. However, on 21st June 1919, German crews decided to start sinking their ships rather than allow the Allies to seize them.

THE HOME FRONT

Although the majority of the fighting during the First World War took place beyond Britain's shores, British people at home were far from unaffected.

THE HOME FRONT

The **Defence of the Realm Act (DORA)** was introduced in August 1914 in the interest of maintaining security during the war. **The Act allowed the government to impose widespread restrictions on the British population, including censorship of newspapers and rationing of food.**

The introduction of food rationing was aimed at preventing panic buying and hoarding of food, thus ensuring there were no food shortages.

However, the supply of food became a national problem from 1916 when German submarines (known as U-boats) began attacking and sinking merchant ships heading for Britain.

The home front in Britain wasn't affected only by Germany's U-boats; there was also a terrifying bombing campaign that saw many towns attacked by German Zeppelins and shelled by warships.

AIR RAIDS

The Zeppelins were capable of carrying up to two tonnes of bombs, and their first campaign in January 1915 targeted Great Yarmouth and King's Lynn. The German air raids resulted in the British authorities imposing 'blackouts' in areas thought to be at risk of attack. Despite such precautions, the raids killed more than 500 British civilians and injured over 1,000.

The bombardment sowed fear among the population, but it may also have contributed to the strong sense of patriotism that sent men flocking in their thousands to the recruiting offices.

British soldiers examine debris from the Zeppelin L32, which was shot down by Frederick Sowrey, RFC, and crashed near Snails Farm, South Green, Great Burstead, near Billericay, Essex, on the night of 23rd–24th September 1916.

PROHIBITION

Throughout the First World War many countries, such as Britain, Germany, Austria-Hungary, France, Russia and Italy, were concerned that the amount of alcohol being consumed by the public was affecting the war effort.

In Britain, Chancellor of the Exchequer David Lloyd George saw alcohol consumption as a huge problem. To address the issue, he started a campaign to encourage national figures to pledge publicly that they would give up alcohol during the war years. One such supporter was King George V, who promised that no alcohol would be drunk in the royal household until the war was over.

The campaign showed little success, and so the 'No Treating Order' was issued, establishing closing times for public houses and preventing people from buying alcoholic drinks for others. Tax on alcohol was increased: by 1918, a bottle of whisky cost five times more than it had before the outbreak of the war. Alcohol consumption was reduced, and British consumption fell from 89 million gallons in 1914 to 37 million gallons in 1918.

The Food Queue by Christopher R W Nevinson (1889–1946). A crowd of grey-faced civilian women, children and men queue in front of a row of shop windows.

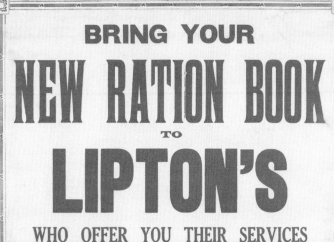

BRING YOUR

NEW RATION BOOK

TO

LIPTON'S

WHO OFFER YOU THEIR SERVICES

The British government introduced rationing in 1918.

What food would you miss most if rationing was introduced now?

DID YOU KNOW...?

IN LONDON IN 1914, 67,000 PEOPLE WERE FOUND GUILTY OF BEING DRUNK. IN 1917 THE NUMBER OF CONVICTIONS HAD FALLEN TO 16,500.

WARTIME WORK

When war broke out in 1914, women in Britain were mainly restricted to lives of domesticity. With so many men going off to war, women were called upon to take their place in factories and other industries.

NEW OPPORTUNITIES

Many women left their low-paid jobs in domestic service for higher-paid work in munitions factories. To keep pace with demand from the front line, this often meant working 12-hour shifts. **Accidents were common in the munitions factories, and dangerous chemicals caused health problems that affected workers long after the war ended.**

Despite their huge contribution from 1914 to 1918, the 1919 Restoration of Pre-War Practices Act forced thousands of women out of their jobs as men came home and factories switched to peacetime production. Overall, the number of women in work actually decreased between 1911 and 1921!

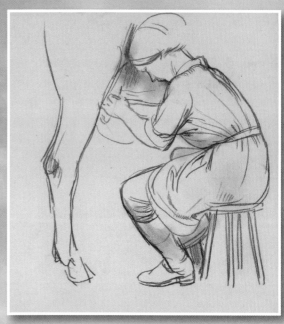

Milking by British artist Randolph Schwabe (1885–1948). A woman of the Women's Land Army sits on a small wooden stool milking a cow.

Shell-Making, Edinburgh by Irish painter John Lavery (1856–1941). A view down the length of a munitions factory. Female workers wearing long overalls and blue hair caps are shown at work manufacturing artillery shells.

My fellow munitionettes and I loved a game of footie (see page 73)!

RATION TINS

Canning factories filled millions of tins with Maconachie's stew, a vital ration which warmed the soldiers who shared mealtimes behind the lines. **Factory workers packed tea, biscuits, chocolates and cigarettes into specially designed and decorated tins to appeal to soldiers at the Front with images of family and home**. However, much of what they kept was ruined by the rain and mud.

TRADE UNIONS

Trade unions became more important than they had ever been before, so important that local trade union representatives were exempt from conscription (see page 11) because they were vital to the war effort. The increase in collective bargaining meant there were far fewer strikes, and in industries that were particularly essential (such as munitions) working conditions improved a lot. **In 1919, more than half of the male work force, and a fifth of the female work force, were members of Trade Unions – more than double the number who were in 1907.**

Echoes Across the Century

In 1917 the harvest failed, leaving Britain with just three weeks' of food reserves. This, combined with the naval blockades by Germany, led the Board of Agriculture to set up the Women's Land Army.

A Land Girl Ploughing by British painter Cecil Aldin (1870–1935).

THE EASTER RISING

Irish nationalists were generally supportive of the British war effort, but a section of the Irish Volunteers (see page 40), comprising about 11,000 men, refused to enlist in the British army and its members continued to parade and drill in Ireland. A number of the volunteers had come under the influence of the Irish Republican Brotherhood (IRB), a secret revolutionary society that saw the world war as an opportunity to stage a republican uprising against British rule in Ireland.

THE EASTER RISING

On Easter Monday in 1916, approximately 1,500 members of the Irish Volunteers, the Irish Citizen Army (ICA, see page 40), and a nationalist women's organisation, Cumann na mBan, took to the streets of Dublin and occupied important buildings around the city centre. **The commander of the rebel forces, Patrick Pearse, declared Ireland an independent republic in front of the General Post Office and the military and political authorities quickly began to mobilise a response.** The republican forces were outnumbered and outgunned, and the British use of artillery meant their positions became indefensible. Pearse surrendered on the sixth day of the battle, by which time almost 500 combatants and civilians had been killed and much of the city centre was in ruins.

Most Irish people either had mixed feelings or were openly hostile toward the rebels and angry about the destruction caused by the rebellion. However, **when the authorities began executing the leaders of the Rising, public opinion became generally more sympathetic towards those, including Patrick Pearse and James Connolly, who had been put to death.**

By the final year of the war, the political party with which the rebels were associated, Sinn Féin, had become the biggest political force in the country.

Birth of the Irish Republic by Walter Paget (1863–1935).

DID YOU KNOW...?

SUFFRAGIST AND PACIFIST CHARLOTTE DESPARD SUPPORTED IRISH HOME RULE. IN 1918, WHEN HER BROTHER, SIR JOHN FRENCH, WAS MADE LORD LIEUTENANT OF IRELAND TO RULE ON BEHALF OF THE KING, THEY WERE IN DIRECT CONFLICT!

CONSTANCE MARKIEVICZ (1868–1927)

Constance Gore-Booth, an Anglo-Irish woman whose family owned land in County Sligo, married a Polish count in 1900 and became known as Countess Markievicz. She came to the attention of British intelligence in 1909 for her role in helping to found a nationalist scouts organisation, Na Fianna Éireann, which was set up to train boys for participation in a war of liberation.

In 1915, she helped to organise and train the Irish Citizen Army (ICA). **During the Easter Rising, Staff Lieutenant Constance Markievicz was second-in-command of a battalion of the ICA**. After the rebels were forced to surrender, she was the only woman to be courtmartialled.

Held in solitary confinement at Kilmainham Gaol, Markievicz heard each of her fellow leaders being shot. The British government decided that it would be too controversial to execute a woman, so she was sentenced to life imprisonment. After serving 13 months, Constance was released.

In the 1918 General Election, **Markievicz was the only woman to be elected MP**. However, in line with Sinn Féin policy, she abstained from taking her seat in the House of Commons.

Studio portrait of Countess Constance Markievicz in uniform with a gun.

POSTWAR

The Sinn Féin party won 73 out of 105 Irish seats in the 1918 General Election, which took place just over a month after the Armistice between Britain and Germany. Sinn Féin MPs refused to recognise the authority of Westminster and decided instead to set up an independent parliament in Dublin.

The Irish War of Independence began in 1919 and eventually led to **the birth of the Irish Free State and the formal division of the island in 1922**. The six counties of the northeast remained within the United Kingdom and became known as Northern Ireland and the remaining 26 counties comprised the Free State, which was declared the Republic of Ireland in 1949. All of these developments meant that the country to which Irish veterans of the world war began returning to in 1919 was very different to the one they had left when they first volunteered to serve.

Constance Markievicz was active in the Irish suffrage movement.

YOUNG PEOPLE AND THE WAR

It was deemed necessary for children to understand why the war effort was so important. In Britain's case, this involved teaching the value of the Empire, both at home and at school. Young people were encouraged to do their bit for the war, whether at home, at school or even on the front line.

WAR IN THE CLASSROOM

Schools and teachers played an important role throughout the First World War. They tried to minimise the physical and psychological threats to their pupils' safety whilst teaching them that the Empire was something worth saving, and stressing that Britain was fighting for the rule of law and for democracy. Teachers were expected to change their curriculum to one that encouraged patriotism and inspired young people to help with the war effort at home.

Schools kept animals and planted gardens in order to encourage children to learn how to farm, for example teaching girls to make jam and to preserve fruit and vegetables for the tougher months. Seeing the benefits, the British government was keen for schools to expand their gardening programmes. By October 1915, 56,037 children were being taught practical gardening in 3,129 school gardens.

British Girl Guides practise semaphore signalling during the war.

DID YOU KNOW...?

GIRLS AND BOYS ALIKE LEARNT FIRST AID DURING THE WAR YEARS. THEY WERE OFTEN EMPLOYED BY HOSPITALS, LOCAL AUTHORITIES AND CENTRAL GOVERNMENT.

Kaiser Bill – *Children's Song*

Kaiser Bill went up the hill
To see the British Army.
General French jumped out of a trench
And made the cows go barmy.

PREPARING FOR WAR

Boy Scouts were taught how to shoot at rifle ranges, a precautionary measure so that they were ready to be called upon to defend Britain if the German army invaded. The War Office used Boy Scouts to guard important places, such as stretches of coastline and railway lines, and taught them to send semaphore messages using small flags. After a long night of guard duty, the Scouts were sometimes allowed the following day off school.

Girl Guides were expected to be able to help the injured after an invasion and to learn useful occupations and handiwork whilst still keeping their womanliness. **Although their training was expected to be done in a feminine way, the Girl Guides adopted uniforms and even had military ranks, which the Boy Scouts did not have.** Some of the girls' activities, such as stealing rival troops' equipment, had to be hidden from the Guiding Headquarters for being too 'unladylike'.

BOY SOLDIERS

For years children had been taught that the Empire was worth protecting and now boys who wanted to fight had their chance to protect it. **Lots of young boys found the prospect of fighting for their country exciting and lied to recruitment officers about their age.**

Cecil Withers joined at 17 and gave a false name and address so that his true age could not be discovered. He then came to realise that if he were to die in battle his family would never be informed. His family thought the same and sent a message through *The Times* in 1916. The message read: 'Cecil C.W. – All's well, will not apply for discharge if you send full address; past forgiven – Father'.

The army employed boys as drummers and buglers, and very often they were the sons of soldiers. In 1914, the War Office ordered all regiments to leave their boys at home, unlike in the South African War (1899–1902), as they were unable to contribute to the campaign. The same did not apply in the Royal Navy, and one boy seaman, Jack Cornwell, won the Victoria Cross at Jutland in 1916 at the age of 16.

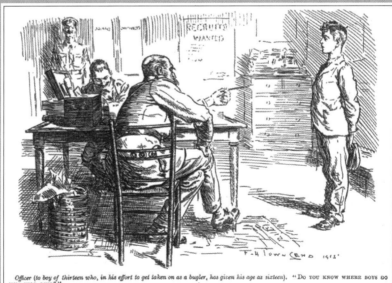

Officer (to boy of thirteen who, in his effort to get taken on as a bugler, has given his age as sixteen). "Do you know where boys go who tell lies?"
Applicant. "To the Front, Sir."

This satirical view of the war by F H Townsend (1868–1920) appeared in *Punch* magazine in 1915.

POETRY FROM THE HOME FRONT

The term 'War Poetry' is now associated with the Soldier Poets of the Great War. People often do not realise that many women and children also wrote poetry. 'Total War' impacts upon everyone's lives, and whether knitting socks, making munitions, seeing the Army requisitioning horses, or mourning loved ones, women and children were fully aware every hour of every day that their nation was at war.

KNITTING POEMS

Yorkshire-born nine-year-old Amy Tyreman, helped by family members including her three-year-old sister who knitted face-cloths, produced 194 articles (mainly socks) for the troops. **In Australia, Nora Pennington won the district record for the number of socks, mufflers, mittens, and balaclavas knitted by anybody under the age of thirteen**.

At school, children used every possible moment to knit, as this poem shows:

> Poetry was sold to raise money for ambulances and for privately run hospitals, and people bought tickets for poetry reading evenings in aid of war causes.

Mary had a Little Lamb
Anonymous Child

Mary had a little lamb
Its fleece was quite expensive,
It followed her to school one day,
And came home feeling pensive.

The little maids at school that day
Forgot their sums and letters.
They pulled the wool all off its back
And knit it into sweaters.

Knitting enabled each woman to connect with her own fighting man. There is something deeply personal about making a garment that a loved one is going to wear next to his skin:

To my Mother – *Anne Page*

On flash her fingers busily, and swift the pattern grows,
And fall the stitches evenly in neatly rounded rows.
And softer eyes are smiling, but they never see at all
The clumsy thread unwinding from the dull, grey worsted ball.
Her shining needles glitter with a thousand mystic gleams –
It isn't wool she's weaving there, it's a gossamer of dreams.

A rosy dream of fights forgot and clouded skies serene,
A white, white dream of honour and a spirit brave and clean.
A thrill of pride, half-fearful, for the strength to do and dare,
A tender little blessing and a quiet little prayer.
And in and out she weaves them from a heart with hope a brim
– It's not a sock she's making, it's a web of love for him.

MUNITIONS POEMS

By the middle of 1915, with more and more men in the Army, women were needed in the factories. **Short though they were of money, many women enthusiastically donated some of their pay to the charities and benevolent funds which sent 'comforts' to men at the Front.** They also invested in War Savings Certificates, despite many of them being unable to afford to eat in the subsidised factory canteens.

This poem was found in a munitions worker's scrapbook:

War Loan – *Unknown*

We're working on munitions to help to win the war,

Now England needs more money, so has called on us once more;

Right gladly would we aid her by giving of our own

That's why we are so busy putting money in War Loan:

So that our gallant fighting men can with conviction say,

'Our women tried to aid us in every possible way.'

from Munitions
Helen Dricks

We have forgotten
the guelder roses,
You and I,
The lilies
And the lilac too;
The sweet scents of Spring
Pass by unnoticed.

My life
Lies in the turning of a lathe
And yours
In the skill to fight –
Two poor cogs in the
machinery of war.

Like the men at the Front, munitions workers were soon caught up in the war machine. **Regulations made it hard to leave a factory or move to an alternate one;** life before the war seemed a distant dream.

WAR SAVINGS CERTIFICATES

Every child can help by buying War Savings Stamps

Boy: *How can we help our Country?*
Girl: *Daddy and I are buying War Savings Stamps. WHY NOT YOU?*

£1 *for* 15/6

Children were encouraged to support the war effort.

Many women suffered from post-traumatic stress disorder following horrific explosions in munitions factories.

OBJECTIONS TO WAR

People all over the world objected to war for different reasons. These included religious and political beliefs, and conscience.

CONSCIENTIOUS OBJECTORS

In 1916, the Military Service Act introduced compulsory military service, known as conscription, to Britain for the first time (see page 11). **Approximately 20,000 men applied for exemption from service because of their beliefs or conscience. They were known as 'Conscientious Objectors'.**

Few who applied on the grounds of conscience were given absolute exemption from service. Some had their applications refused and were sent to fight, and others were required to undertake work of national importance or non-combatant roles, such as joining the Royal Army Medical Corps or the newly formed Non-Combatant Corps.

There were many reasons why men objected to military service. For some it was a religious one, for instance some took 'Thou shalt not kill' in the Bible at its word. For others it was political or because they did not agree with government intervention.

Poster published by the Parliament and Joint Labour Recruiting Committee, London.

TRIBUNALS

Men could be exempted from conscription only by applying to a tribunal. Reasons for applying to a tribunal varied from moral grounds (conscientious objectors), family grounds (looking after dependents), medical grounds (disability) or economic grounds (preserving a business such as farming or mills). Most of the men who applied to a tribunal did so for economic reasons.

Tribunals were held in town halls, parish churches and local schools, and were made up of local dignitaries who often had little or no legal experience. Absolute exemption from military service was possible; however, this was rare. In most cases, the appeals were dismissed by tribunal members and applicants would go on to take up combatant or non-combatant roles.

There were sensitive issues surrounding conscription, including a stigma toward those who did not serve, so the government instructed local government boards to destroy all tribunal material. Only records from Middlesex, Lothian and Peebles remain. As most of the tribunal papers were destroyed after the war, the exact number of men exempted, either temporarily or completely, from compulsory service is not known. However, it is estimated that approximately 1.5 million men had been exempted.

> The non-combatant corps was a military unit which supported the war without fighting or the use of arms.

What would you draw on your cell wall?

RICHMOND CASTLE

In 1916, Richmond Castle in North Yorkshire became a base for the northern companies of the Non-Combatant Corps. Most men sent to Richmond accepted non-combatant work, **but some refused to follow military orders**. Men who refused to follow military orders were called 'absolutists' and were often detained in harsh conditions.

Covering the fragile walls of the 19th-century cell block are thousands of pieces of graffiti, including many drawn by conscientious objectors. The walls of the cells are covered with a range of inscriptions, including Biblical verses, Socialist slogans, illustrations of loved ones, and political or religious affiliations.

'You might just as well try to dry a floor by throwing water on it as try to end this war by fighting' – by Richard Lewis Barry, a Socialist conscientious objector who worked in a lace factory in Derbyshire.

THE RICHMOND 16

In May 1916, 16 conscientious objectors detained at Richmond Castle were sent with serving members of the Non-Combatant Corps to France. **These men have become known as the 'Richmond 16'.**

Among them was Norman Gaudie, a reserve Sunderland footballer who believed that participation in war went against his Congregationalist faith, and John Hubert Brocklesby, a schoolteacher who argued that fighting broke the Sixth Commandment – 'Thou Shalt not kill'.

In France, the Richmond 16 continued to resist their enlistment

John Hubert Brocklesby, one of the 'Richmond Sixteen', drew this portrait of his fiancée Annie Wainright on his cell wall. At a later date the inscription was re-labelled 'My Kathleen'.

and refused an order to move supplies. They were courtmartialled in front of a huge crowd, found guilty and sentenced to death. This was then reduced to 10 years' imprisonment with hard labour.

MEDIA & PROPAGANDA

The use of media and propaganda during the First World War served a multitude of purposes. It was not only used to encourage young men to sign up to the army, it also aimed to keep morale high, and maintain the nation's will to fight.

RECRUITMENT CAMPAIGNS

The best-known campaign was that of Lord Kitchener's appeal for volunteers to sign up to the army. Lord Kitchener was Secretary of State for War and had been a career soldier; he believed that the war would last up to four years and that millions of men would need to be mobilised to win it. Therefore he created a new volunteer army – **soldiers had to be at least 18 years old to join, and 19 before they could be sent abroad to fight.**

Due to Lord Kitchener's recruitment campaigns, it was realised that more men joined if they were able to serve alongside their friends and relatives. And so, **to encourage friends to join together, Lord Kitchener's Pal Battalion recruitment campaign was created**. On 21st August 1914 the first Pals Battalion was raised from stockbrokers in London. The first of the battalions began arriving on the Western Front after training in the middle of August 1915. A direct consequence of such battalions was that there were disproportionate losses among some villages and towns as these Pals died together. Some villages lost nearly all the men who joined up. Others lost none.

Propaganda poster

Crowd of rioters breaking the windows of a German-owned shop in East London, following the sinking of the *Lusitania* on 7th May 1915.

DID YOU KNOW...?

THE *TRIBUNAL* NEWSPAPER WAS PUBLISHED FROM 1916 TO 1919 BY THE NO-CONSCRIPTION FELLOWSHIP. IT INCLUDED PIECES ON THE EXPERIENCES OF CONSCIENTIOUS OBJECTORS, AND OPINION ARTICLES ON CONSCRIPTION. THE PAPER WAS UNDER CONSTANT THREAT OF CENSORSHIP BY THE BRITISH GOVERNMENT.

PROPAGANDA TECHNIQUES

As the government became more desperate for help toward the war effort, they developed new techniques in the hope that their message would reach all.

Perception of the Enemy

Germany was portrayed as death and destruction in Britain. The nation was seen as a dangerous enemy that was killing their men and had to be defeated. This technique became problematic as there were over 50,000 Germans living in Britain. Throughout the war, there was lots of anti-German sentiment in national newspapers and propaganda which on occasion made direct links between Germans living in Britain and the actions of the German Army. Anti-German riots broke out after Zeppelin air raids, and when a German U-boat sank the *Lusitania* many German businesses came under attack.

National Pride

The war was portrayed as a group effort; every person was faced with loss, so felt they had to play their part. There was one shared goal, and that was winning the war and protecting Britain. People were encouraged to see what their neighbours and friends were doing. The message was clear, if everyone got together, they could win.

Media

Posters and newspapers were also used to encourage men to volunteer for the war effort. Posters targeted women and children in the hope that they would persuade more men to join the army. They also appealed to women to join the Women's Land Army, and non-combatant organisations such as the Women's Army Auxiliary Corps (WAAC, see page 20).

CENSORSHIP

Defeat in conflict is not confined to the battlefield; maintaining a nation's will to fight is just as important as having a strong army. **The British government dealt with domestic dissent by setting up the National War Aims Committee (NWAC) in 1917 as a semi-official group to craft and distribute pro-war messages**. To help politicians deny that they were stifling free speech, the NWAC paid freelance journalists and worked with unions, labour organisations and church groups to tailor what was said to the public.

How would you feel if you found out that the government was stifling freedom of speech in Britain today?

POETRY & POETS

WILFRED OWEN (1893-1918)

Wilfred Owen described himself as a 'pacifist with a seared conscience'. He enlisted in the British army in 1915 and first arrived in France in January 1917. He spent the next few months serving at Serre and St Quentin, but was sent back to Britain for treatment for shell shock in April 1917. **Under the guidance and encouragement of Siegfried Sassoon, Wilfred wrote with a burning honesty about the horrific reality of the war**. He hated it, and in his poetry he explored and described the true horrors and trauma of war and the experiences of the common soldier. 'Dulce et Decorum Est' is a war poem in which he describes a gas attack.

He returned to France in August 1918 and took part in the breaking of the Hindenburg Line in October of the same year, for which he was awarded the Military Cross. He was killed on 4th August 1918 whilst leading his men across the Sambre-Oise Canal. The telegram to his mother saying Wilfred was dead arrived as the church bells were ringing out to celebrate the Armistice.

Dulce et Decorum Est – *Wilfred Owen*

Bent double, like old beggars under sacks,
Knock-kneed, coughing like hags, we cursed through sludge,
Till on the haunting flares we turned our backs
And towards our distant rest began to trudge.
Men marched asleep. Many had lost their boots
But limped on, blood-shod. All went lame; all blind;
Drunk with fatigue; deaf even to the hoots
Of tired, outstripped Five-Nines that dropped behind.

Gas! Gas! Quick, boys!---An ecstasy of fumbling,
Fitting the clumsy helmets just in time;
But someone still was yelling out and stumbling,
And flound'ring like a man in fire or lime...
Dim, through the misty panes and thick green light
As under a green sea, I saw him drowning.

In all my dreams, before my helpless sight,
He plunges at me, guttering, choking, drowning.

If in some smothering dreams you too could pace
Behind the wagon that we flung him in,
And watch the white eyes writhing in his face,
His hanging face, like a devil's sick of sin;
If you could hear, at every jolt, the blood
Come gargling from the froth-corrupted lungs,
Obscene as cancer, bitter as the cud
Of vile, incurable sores on innocent tongues,---
My friend, you would not tell with such high zest
To children ardent for some desperate glory,
The old Lie: Dulce et decorum est
Pro patria mori.

'Dulce et decorum est pro patria mori' is Latin for 'it is sweet and right to die for your country'.

ISAAC ROSENBERG (1890-1918)

Isaac Rosenberg was the son of Russian Jewish immigrants, and was a keen and talented painter. In 1914, he was sent to South Africa to stay with his sister for health reasons. Isaac was thought a better painter than a poet in his day, but he was hopelessly chaotic in his personal habits. **Returning from South Africa, he ruined a large number of paintings by stacking them whilst still wet touching each other, and then dropped some over the side when his ship docked at Southampton.**

Isaac returned to England in March 1915 and enlisted in the British Army. **He found army life very hard; he was passed from one unit to another, and was victimised because of his faith and artistic temperament.** He wrote many of his poems whilst fighting in the trenches on the Western Front and is known for his great use of imagination. In March 1918, he was killed whilst on patrol during the German army's spring offensive. His body was never found.

SIEGFRIED SASSOON (1886-1967)

Siegfried Sassoon arrived in France with the British army in May 1915 where he gained the name 'Mad Jack' for his bravery on the battlefield. Influenced and encouraged by pacifist friends such as the philosopher Bertrand Russell, Siegfried decided to make a stand against the war by writing a letter to a British newspaper in 1917. This act by a serving officer could have been met with severe punishment, and even the death sentence. However, his friend and fellow war poet Robert Graves convinced the military authorities that Siegfried was suffering from shell shock, and the Army itself did not wish to create a martyr to the pacifist cause.

Siegfried was subsequently sent to Craiglockhart war hospital in Edinburgh, where he helped fellow patients with their writing, including Wilfred Owen. When he returned to fight in the war he was posted first to Palestine and then to France, before returning to Britain for the remainder of the conflict after being wounded in the trenches. He wrote poetry throughout the First World War and published a number of volumes after the Armistice.

MUSIC IN THE WAR

Humanity creates music around and for all great events, and the First World War was no exception. There are three main groups of music associated with the war: classical music, music hall music and marching songs.

CLASSICAL MUSIC

Much of the 'classical' genre was written after the war. The most modern, and probably the best known, is the *War Requiem* by Benjamin Britten. Written in 1961, this masterpiece was influenced by the poems of Wilfred Owen (see page 106).

Some First World War poems have been set to music as songs. A very famous example inspired by the events of the First World War was Edward Elgar's Cello Concerto.

Christmas Night, Cassel, 1917 by William Orpen. Cassel was a town in the Ypres Salient, Belgium, where soldiers could come away from the fighting. Here, Orpen observed, they could 'eat, drink, play the piano and sing, forgetting their misery and discomfort for the moment... One saw gaiety, misery, fear, thoughtfulness and unthoughtfulness all mixed up like a kaleidoscope.'

IVOR GURNEY

Ivor Gurney, a student of the Royal College of Music, is famous for composing music during the war. Ivor's piece 'Severn Meadows' was inspired by his time as a private serving with the Gloucestershire Regiment. **Initially rejected due to his poor eyesight, Ivor joined the 2nd and 5th Gloucestershire Regiment in 1915.** He was injured in April 1917, suffered from a gas attack in September of the same year and was subsequently sent home. Ivor had a history of mental illness which affected him severely in the postwar years; he continued to write poetry and compose music during this time.

Severn Meadows
Ivor Gurney (1890–1937)

Only the wanderer
Knows England's graces,
Or can anew see clear
　　Familiar faces.

And who loves joy as he
That dwells in shadows?
Do not forget me quite,
　　O Severn meadows.

The grave of Ivor Gurney at Twigworth, Gloucestershire.

What would your soldier song be?

MUSIC HALL

The main form of entertainment during the war was Music Hall. It was a live show in front of a live audience, and the performers were the stars and celebrities of the day. These songs were for a civilian audience, so they were often cheery, optimistic and sentimental. One of the most famous examples of the type was 'Keep the Home Fires Burning'. **The songs had to be optimistic; if they had told the truth about the suffering of the soldiers, the government would have banned them immediately!** Yet these songs are remembered as symbolising the feelings of ordinary people at home during the war. However, they were often rejected by the soldiers at the front, who used the tunes of the popular music hall songs but invented their own, often very rude, alternative words. One example is the famous song 'It's A Long Way To Tipperary', with the first line, 'It's a long way to Tipperary, It's a long way to go'. If you heard it at all on the front line, it would have been turned into, 'That's not the way to tickle Mary, that's not how you go…' The people at home were comforted by the cheerful music hall songs, and rarely, if ever, heard the rude versions sung by the soldiers!

MARCHING SONGS

In 1914–18, a soldier got around by walking – except groups of soldiers do not walk to places. They march, in unison, together. Singing together as a group helped the men to keep time and beat out a rhythm for them to march to. **Unfortunately, most of the marching songs are too rude to reproduce here!**

Soldiers, sailors, and airman used 'soldier songs' to strengthen morale and bond together in the face of the bleak life at war. Much of the light verse or songs sung by them did not focus on blood and guts. They had enough of that in reality, and didn't need to be reminded. Their music and songs were not only functional (marching songs do actually help you to march), but they also boosted morale of the soldiers!

Bagpipers march through an unidentified town in Flanders. This is one of several sketches of the First World War by British artist Gertrude Leese (1870–1963).

CARTOONS

Since the 19th century, cartoons have been used as humorous illustrations in magazines and newspapers. During the First World War cartoons were used to ridicule the German threat and to boost morale. Newspapers and magazines were subject to government censorship, so cartoons were limited in their capacity to criticise the war. However, the 'comic' nature of cartoons meant that they were able to get much closer to the reality of conflict than any other form of art or journalism.

BRUCE BAIRNSFATHER (1887-1959)

Captain Bruce Bairnsfather went to France in November 1914 as a Machine Gun Officer with the 1st Royal Warwickshire Regiment. He participated in the famous 1914 Christmas Truce, and was wounded in the Second Battle of Ypres on 25th April 1915.

Bruce sent his first sketch to *The Bystander* magazine in March 1915, and his cartoons caught the imagination of men on the front line and their families back home. He soon became a household name, and published volumes of his 'Fragments from France' cartoons sold over a million copies. His cartoons appeared on merchandise, including postcards, prints, jigsaws, playing cards and even a range of Bairnsfather Ware china. **His most famous character was a walrus-moustached old soldier called Old Bill**.

In 1916, Bruce was transferred to the Intelligence Department of the War Office, and appointed 'Officer Cartoonist', touring the French, Italian and American fronts at the request of the Allied armies. By 1918 he had become the most famous cartoonist of his time, credited by General Sir Ian Hamilton as 'the man who made the world laugh in its darkest hour'.

"Well, if you knows of a better 'ole, go to it."

A typical Bairnsfather cartoon. Old Bill is the character on the left.

"They've evidently seen me."

Bairnsfather showed the funny side of adversity.

ARCHIE GILKISON (1885-1916)

Born in Glasgow, Archie Gilkison wrote and cartooned under the nickname 'Baldy' for newspapers including *The Glasgow Herald*, *The Evening Times*, the Dundee *Courier*, London Opinion and the Bristol *Echo*. He also illustrated books.

Though Gilkison is best known for humour and wit, the war brought out a more serious and patriotic side to his art. **From 1914 to 1916 he produced hundreds of cartoons, many focusing on the darkest elements of war – death, destruction and retribution**. His work is erudite, referencing Shakespeare, the classical world and current affairs, and much of it is sharply ironic.

Following the rediscovery of his work in 2014, Archie, who was self-taught,

has been described as 'the Wilfred Owen of cartooning' – he is the only popular cartoonist known to have depicted the horrors of the war while it was ongoing.

Archie was perhaps at the height of his cartooning career just as he was conscripted into the Scots Guards in October 1916, despite having been rejected on medical grounds in 1914 due to life-long respiratory problems. During training in Berwick, a chill Archie caught developed into pneumonia and he died aged 31 on 2nd November of that year, never having made it to the front line.

The Reason Why

"I know that my glorious Western Army will never retreat"
—*German Emperor's message to his troops in the West*

Archie Gilkison's style and quality of line drawing were exceptional. He was often ahead of his time, as evidenced here, in his sketch which depicts the corpse of a German soldier lying rotting in a trench. The work could easily be mistaken for something drawn decades later.

THE WIPERS TIMES

The Wipers Times was a trench magazine named after the army slang for the Belgian city of Ypres. It was a satirical publication offering a release from the misery of the conflict through songs, puns and literary parodies, all of which proved popular with the troops.

> The name 'Wipers' was used by Field Marshal Sir John French because he couldn't pronounce 'Ypres'.

HOSPITALS

The First World War was a new kind of war; hospitals and medical personnel had to adapt and advance quickly to save the seriously wounded. The war witnessed an unprecedented number of casualties: in total, around nine million soldiers died, and more than twice that number were wounded.

THE CHAIN OF EVACUATION

The chain of evacuation was created to manage the mass of injuries caused by fighting on the front line, and to save as many lives as possible. **At each stage a professional could decide if the injured soldier could rejoin his regiment or needed further help**. Evacuation back home for treatment was not simple, and there was not one set method. Sometimes stretchers and horses were used (see page 26), and sometimes hospital trains and ships were created!

TRANSPORTING THE WOUNDED

Ambulances: Motorised ambulances were used for the first time during the First World War. The Red Cross established a motor ambulance department which resulted in a fleet of over 3,400 motor vehicles including over 2,000 motor ambulances. Motorised ambulances became the preferred method of transporting the wounded as opposed to horse ambulances. Many of the drivers were cabbies from London.

Trains: After treatment in a Casualty Clearing Station, if deemed necessary, men could be loaded onto trains with hospital beds and equipment. This way they could quickly get to a base hospital or near to the French coast, if the injury needed specialist treatment. The British initially used old French trains, but as time went on they began to build their own. The mobile hospitals proved useful and popular – they increased chances of survival and became a key way of drumming up charitable donations back home!

Ships: The Red Cross and the Army Medical Services worked together for the first time in 1898 to transport wounded via the sea. Motor launches, which were small military vessels, were used as hospital ships to serve Mesopotamia (see page 51) during 1915. By the end of 1916, 33 British Red Cross launches were in operation in Mesopotamia. The Red Cross also had a river hospital ship, *Nahba*, which carried patients between Basra and Baghdad from May 1917.

Étaples Hospital Siding by Olive Mudie-Cooke (1890–1925), a British artist who worked as an ambulance driver in northern France.

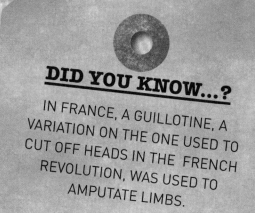

DID YOU KNOW...?

IN FRANCE, A GUILLOTINE, A VARIATION ON THE ONE USED TO CUT OFF HEADS IN THE FRENCH REVOLUTION, WAS USED TO AMPUTATE LIMBS.

3RD AUSTRALIAN GENERAL HOSPITAL (3AGH)

The British War Office knew that medical care was urgently needed at Gallipoli, so asked the well-known Italian surgeon Thomas Henry Fiaschi to set up the 3rd Australian General Hospital (3AGH). 3AGH helped Allied troops and injured patients all over the world.

The first was established on the Greek island of Lemnos, and, on 8th August 1915, 40 nurses from the Australian Army Nursing Service (AANS, see page 57) arrived. **They received around 200 wounded from Gallipoli on the first day, and that total increased to over 800 in just a few days**. Thousands were wounded and brought to the hospital but only 33 men died from their injuries or disease! Although the Allied troops left Gallipoli in December 1915, the hard-working hospital staff did not stop work there. They moved to Cairo, Egypt, in January 1916, where they treated 7,400 patients, of whom only 143 died. The success of 3AGH continued until the end of the war with their bases in England and France.

Drawing of the 3rd AGH in Abbeville, France, 1918 by Arthur Streeton (1867–1943). In 1918 while based in London, Arthur was appointed by the Australian War Memorial as an official war artist to record the involvement of his fellow Australians in the battles taking place along the Somme River.

INDIAN HOSPITALS

Brighton was chosen as the site for the first set of hospitals in Britain dedicated to the care of wounded and sick Indian soldiers. The town authorities gave three buildings for this purpose: the workhouse (renamed the Kitchener Hospital), the York Place School and the Royal Pavilion.

The Royal Pavilion was the first hospital to open, with its first patients arriving in early December 1914. Efforts were made to accommodate the religious and cultural needs of the men, with a tented gurdwara in the grounds of the Pavilion for Sikhs, and space on the eastern lawns for Muslims to pray facing Mecca. Separate kitchens were also established to meet the religious dietary requirements of the men. Brighton's Indian hospitals gradually closed towards the end of 1915 as the British started to withdraw Indian infantry from Europe and redeploy them to the Middle East.

Indian Army Wounded In Hospital in the Dome, Brighton by Douglas Fox Pitt (1864–1922).

ADVANCEMENTS IN MEDICINE

The number and variety of casualties in the First World War were not seen before. Because of a new kind of warfare (see page 18), medical professionals had to adapt and improve their abilities to treat all types of injuries. The Western Front faced an unimaginable scale of wounded soldiers, and they had to deal with various physical and mental injuries. Medical advancements and the ability to transport critical medical equipment to the front line saved many lives!

BLOOD TRANSFUSION

One of the most common effects of injury was bleeding. Blood loss can be extremely dangerous, so dealing with it quickly was vital to saving the patient's life. With an increasing number of men dying as a result of blood loss, doctors knew that something had to change.

Throughout the war, treating blood loss proved a challenge, but **in 1918 Oswald Hope Robertson managed to create a working method of blood transfusion, which increased the chances of survival**. Not only did he create a better working transfusion apparatus, he also discovered how to store blood for longer than ever before. His transportable medical invention allowed blood transfusions to happen on the front line. Doctors also needed plenty of blood in storage to be able to carry out transfusions, which led to the introduction of 'blood banks'.

TREATING GAS WOUNDS

A new war technique was exposing the enemy to poisonous gasses. Throughout the First World War, both treatments for and protection against gas attacks greatly improved, such as the gas mask. However, a gas attack was still a horrific experience, with many lasting physical and mental effects. **Poisonous gases could take hours to kill their victims. One method of treatment was artificially increasing oxygen in the patient's blood**.

John Scott Haldane travelled to the Western Front soon after the first gas attack to help save as many lives as he could. He invented an apparatus that helped to increase the level of oxygen in the patient's blood, and protective equipment, which was very important as he was exposed to the poisonous gas himself. John's apparatus allowed four people to be treated at the same time. As the war went on, it was increasingly regarded as an essential piece of medical equipment, and was supplied to special gas treatment units near the front line.

A Royal Army Medical Corps officer tends a group of wounded Turks on stretchers with the assistance of some Indian staff at an advanced dressing station after the British capture of Tikrit in Mesopotamia in 1917.

BERT FEARNS (1897–1997)

Bert Fearns of the 6th Lancashire Fusiliers stands out within the context of sight loss and the City of Liverpool. **Bert was badly wounded by shell fire in March 1918** during the German 'last gasp' offensive, losing one eye. **When Bert was about to be bayoneted, the German trooper noticed that he was a Lancashire Fusilier and took pity on him**. The German soldier had served at the Adelphi Hotel in Liverpool before the outbreak of war, and had liked the Liverpool people. The German soldier took it upon himself to bandage Bert up and take him prisoner, rather than deliver the coup de grâce. Bert became a prisoner of war, but survived and was returned to his family in the UK.

VISUAL IMPAIRMENT

The First World War resulted in thousands of soldiers losing their sight due to gas, bullets, explosions, shell fire and disease. Visual impairment proved tricky, and doctors could not cure the blindness that so many men experienced. Instead, they could provide artificial eyes, but sadly these were in very short supply. **There began to be a huge demand for artificial eyes, but as most of them were produced in Germany, Britain did not have access to these**. The supply that Britain did have was given to the Army Spectacle Depot to distribute, and from December 1916 to August 1919 the Army Spectacle Depot provided 22,000 artificial eyes across Britain!

One thing that visually impaired men needed was the ability to live an independent life. After losing their sight, they would have felt that they could no longer do simple things like tell the time. This led to the creation of devices to help blinded soldiers complete day-to-day tasks, including the Braille watch. This watch had raised features so that the time could be known just by touch! Devices like the Braille watch were an important step for these men towards regaining their confidence and independence.

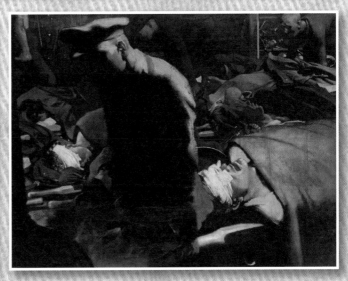

Gassed and Wounded by English artist Eric Henri Kennington (1888–1960).

Many children, including Boy Scouts and Girl Guides, searched for sphagnum moss during the First World War. It was mass-produced as a dressing to help the injured soldiers!

NURSING

During the First World War, huge developments were made in medicine (see page 114). Medical professions also changed considerably, particularly nursing. The high number of casualties meant that more women than ever were training as nurses and travelling far from home to work in often very dangerous conditions.

FIRST AID NURSING YEOMANRY (FANY)

The First Aid Nursing Yeomanry (FANY) was founded in 1907 as an all-women uniformed organisation, created by a Boer War veteran to provide the 'missing link somewhere in the Ambulance Department'. It was decided that 'each member of the Corps would receive… training… so that [they] could ride onto the battlefield to attend the wounded who might otherwise have been left to a slow death'.

The original caption of this cartoon read: 'The Adjutant-General asks the FANY if they can extend their activities'.

In spite of official resistance from the British War Office, the first group of FANYs arrived in Calais on 27th October 1914. The Belgian Army, forced to retreat to the coast, welcomed them with open arms. In spite of often meeting hostility and male opposition to women being so near to the front line, for the next four years FANY continued to run hospitals and convalescent homes. They also drove and maintained ambulances, supply lorries and staff cars for the Belgian and French Armies. **On 1st January 1916, they became the first women to drive officially for the British Army**.

The FANYs served all over the Western Front, and were awarded many decorations for gallantry and service, including the Military Medal, the Légion d'honneur, the Croix de guerre and the Ordre de Leopold II.

The FANY is still an all-women voluntary organisation which supports the civil and military authorities within the United Kingdom during major incidents and public events. To find out more about the history of the FANY, please visit **www.fany.org.uk**

Find out more about the Australian Army Nursing Service on page 59!

THE ENDELL STREET WOMEN'S 'SUFFRAGETTE' HOSPITAL

In September 1914, two suffragettes set off for France. They were Louisa, daughter of Elizabeth Garrett Anderson (England's first-ever woman doctor) and her colleague, Flora Murray. As the British Royal Army Medical Corps (RAMC) refused to accept women doctors, they had offered their services to the French Red Cross and were heading to Paris to establish the Women's Hospital Corps (WHC).

RAMC medics who visited the WHC hospital were amazed! They asked the women to work with the British Army in Boulogne. One patient was a former policeman who remembered arresting suffragette Louisa! The big breakthrough came in February 1915, when they were asked to establish an RAMC hospital in London's Endell Street. The Women's 'Suffragette' Hospital was born.

Entirely staffed by women, the hospital was one of the most successful in England with a much lower than average mortality rate and patients eager to be admitted there. They also managed a bit of quiet propaganda for Votes for Women. One soldier was so impressed by his 'lady doctors' that he wanted them to have ten votes each.

Oh you criticise the clothes,
or lack of them, as worn
by members of the female sex
who rise at early dawn.
And carry on throughout the day
to help this stinking war.
Just try to think, a thing I feel
you've never done before.
We're sorry if our garb offends.
We do not like your smile
when you observe a skirt that reaches
to the knee only of our breeches.
We do not wear for choice, you see
these clothes utilitarian.
We hate our nails to be unkept,
our hair like a barbarian.

So do not blame us overmuch.
We're useful, we believe.
And for a precedent we show
the costume worn by Eve.
For when engaged in useful work
After 'the fall', they say
The clothing worn by Eve was not
What people wear today.
Diane Paynter

Diane Paynter was an early and long-serving FANY, Corps number 136. She was a driver in Calais, France, and was made Lance Corporal. She was Mentioned in Dispatches (MID) for bravery in 1918.

The Workroom of the Gerrard's Cross War Hospital Supply Depôt by English painter Joseph Barnard Davis (1861–1943).

NURSING STORIES

EDITH CAVELL

Died: 12.10.1915
Commemorated: Norwich Cathedral and St Martin's Place, London

Edith was born in Norfolk to a vicar with strong Anglican values. She trained to be a nurse relatively late in life, but soon made a considerable contribution to the nursing profession and was praised for her commitment to patient care. After her training in London, she worked in various UK hospitals before being asked to nurse a sick child in Belgium. Her skills were noticed, and she was invited to be the first matron at Belgium's first nursing school and hospital.

At the outbreak of the First World War, Edith was visiting her mother in Norfolk and, against her mother's wishes, returned to Belgium to help those injured during the conflict. **Edith remained in Belgium working for the Red Cross, caring for both Allied and German injured soldiers, and it was during this time that she started giving Allied soldiers shelter and helping them to escape as part of the resistance movement**. After helping over 200 Allied troops escape to neutral Holland, Edith was betrayed and arrested. She was tried along with 30 others on charges of assisting the enemy. She was found guilty of treason and, despite international pressure, was executed by firing squad on 12th October 1915. The death sentence was carried out only on Edith and one other and caused international outrage, further shaping public opinion in Canada and the United States about entering the war.

Edith is perhaps most remembered for her last words to her chaplain the night before her execution: 'Patriotism is not enough, I must have no hatred or bitterness to anyone', the words are inscribed on her memorial in St Martin's Place, London. After the war, her body was transferred from Belgium to the UK and she was given a state funeral in Westminster Abbey before her body was transferred to her final resting place in Norwich Cathedral.

Drawing by Edith Cavell.

Cavell Nurses' Trust was established from public donations in response to Edith's execution in 1917 and exists as her legacy of caring and learning. For full details, please visit **www.cavellnursestrust.org**

KATHLEEN ADELE BRENNAN

Died: 24.11.1918
Commemorated: Welford Road Cemetery, Leicester

Kathleen Adele Brennan was born in Sydney on 15th November 1882, the eldest of five children. On the outbreak of the First World War, it was agreed that while all five children wanted to serve, one girl and one boy would need to remain in Australia to look after their elderly parents, solicitor William Francis Brennan and his wife Elizabeth Mary Brennan.

Kathleen was allowed to go, and she became a member of the Voluntary Aid Detachment (VAD) with the Australian Red Cross.

She left Australia in September 1916 on board the SS *Osterley* and on arrival in **England was posted to the 5th Northern General Hospital in Leicester.** She served there until just after the end of the war in November 1918, when she died from septic pericarditis following a bout of influenza.

The coffin, which was covered with a Union Jack, was borne to the cemetery on a gun carriage, followed by a large procession of the Royal Army Medical Corps staff and VAD nurses from North Evington and the base hospitals. Her body was interred in the soldiers' corner of the cemetery.

A party from Glen Parva Barracks fired three volleys and the 'Last Post' was sounded by RAMC buglers.

AGNES FLORIEN FORNERI

Died: 24.04.1918
Commemorated: Bramshott Military Cemetery

Agnes Florien Forneri was born 18th April 1881 in Belleville, Ontario, the third of six children of Richard Sykes Forneri, an Anglican priest, and Kate McDermott.

Forneri trained at the nursing school at the Lady Stanley Institute in Ottawa, and graduated in 1906.

She volunteered for the Canadian Army Medical Corps in early 1917. Her brother, David Alwyn, was serving in France, but unfortunately was killed in action one month before she reached England. **She served first at the Kitchener Military Hospital as a volunteer in February 1917, and then at No 8 Canadian General Hospital at Saint-Cloud, a suburb of Paris.**

In January 1918, Forneri fell ill with bronchitis, and returned to England for convalescence. She recovered, and returned to service at the No 12 Canadian General Hospital in Bramshott.

On 17 April

> **NURSE FOLLOWS BROTHER**
>
> **Daughter of Canon Forneri Dies Overseas—Son Killed in Action.**
>
> From Our Own Correspondent.
>
> Kingston, April 27.—The death occurred at Bramshott Canadian Hospital, England, on the 24th April of Nursing Sister Forneri, eldest daughter of Canon Forneri, of Kingston. She had been overseas a year and served for some time in France. Her brother, Lieut. D. A. Forneri, of Montreal, was killed in action a year ago.
>
> *Toronto Evening Telegram - April 27th, 1918*

1918 she collapsed while on duty in the hospital due to a stomach haemorrhage. She underwent an operation, but died on 24th April from multiple peptic ulcers.

FACIALLY INJURED

Soldiers had to lift their heads above the trenches to see across the battlefield. This made them vulnerable to attack from an array of weapons, and they often suffered serious injuries and wounds to the face and head as a result.

FACIALLY INJURED

The dressing stations and hospitals behind the lines on both sides at the Battle of the Somme (see page 12) had never before seen so many men with severe facial injuries. On both sides, governments were forced to bring together the most ingenious surgeons of the day and the early pioneers of plastic surgery to tackle the challenge.

On the Allied side in the early days of the war, the British New Zealander Ear, Nose and Throat (ENT) surgeon Harold Gillies worked with Charles Auguste Valadier, a French-American dentist in Boulogne who had set up a small facial injury service, and French surgeon Hippolyte Morrestin to invent new techniques for closing facial wounds and treating the loss of skin and tissue. On the German side, Fedor Krause, Jacques Joseph, August Lindemann and other surgical colleagues were facing similar challenges.

Gillies was shocked by the injuries he saw in the field, and requested that the army set up their own plastic surgery unit. In June 1917, the new Queen's Hospital (later Queen Mary's Hospital) opened in Sidcup, Kent, in response to the huge number of facially wounded soldiers. The hospital specialised in facial reconstruction. Here Gillies and his colleagues developed many techniques of plastic surgery. **More than 11,000 operations were performed on over 5,000 men, mostly with facial injuries.**

HENRY TONKS

In early 1916, Harold Gillies enlisted Henry Tonks, who had trained as a doctor and was Assistant Professor of Art at the Slade School of Art in London, to draw his patients at Aldershot Hospital and then later at Sidcup. **Tonks was asked to produce diagrams of the operations so that Gillies would be able to see his patients' injuries before and after surgery, and reflect on what the surgeons had done**.

Tonks's pastels are the finest examples of medical imaging before the advent of medical photography, but he viewed them as unacceptable for public view.

Portrait of a Wounded Soldier before Treatment by Henry Tonks (1862–1937).

The same artist's *Portrait of a Wounded Soldier after Treatment*, 1916–17.

> Many facial injuries were caused by shrapnel.

120

Steel helmets were adopted in 1915–16 to address the problem of head injuries.

POST-SURGERY

In Britain, even after Gillies and his team had done their best to treat these soldiers' damaged faces with the new plastic surgery methods, their faces were almost completely hidden from view:

- Mirrors were removed from the wards where they were treated
- They were physically, psychologically and socially isolated from other patients, the world beyond the hospital's extensive grounds, and also from their families who sometimes, it is reported, did not want to see them
- Prosthetic masks were developed to cover their damaged facial features
- In spite of journalistic claims for near-miraculous restoration through modern surgical methods, unofficial censorship in the British press ensured images of facially wounded veterans were not shown – whereas amputees were celebrated as war heroes.

British veterans who had sustained facial injuries often returned home and resumed their prewar occupations or worked in new trades or acquired new skills through the extensive rehabilitation facilities at Sidcup.

Many thousands of French soldiers were also facially wounded in the trenches. They went on to form an organisation called Les Gueules Cassées (The Shattered Faces). Their charity appeals, which included images of soldiers with facial injuries, attracted huge funds with which they bought and established a grand house offering members treatment and convalescence.

Among the thousands of facially wounded French soldiers was Gaston Julia, originally from Algeria, and conscripted at the age of 21. Gaston's facial injury destroyed his nose. His numerous surgeries were unsuccessful, and he wore a leather cover over the part of his face where his nose had been. Gaston had a long and successful career as a top mathematician.

Saline Infusion: An incident in the British Red Cross Hospital, Arc-en-Barrois, 1915 by Henry Tonks. A patient undergoes a saline infusion on a hospital ward in northern France.

Gaston Julia (right) with German mathematician and colleague, Gustav Herglotz.

HUNDRED DAYS OFFENSIVE

The Hundred Days or 'Advance to Victory' was the final campaign of the First World War on the Western Front. The Allies were able to capitalise on gambles made by German forces in a series of offensives beginning in March 1918 and running through to July. German forces focused their attention westwards in an attempt to defeat the Allies before the Americans joined the fighting. However, they suffered heavy losses and their gains extended their line, leaving them with too much to hold with too few men. These offensives in late September attacked the Central Powers from different points of the compass, preventing them from reinforcing one front from another.

BATTLE OF AMIENS

On 24th July 1918, the Allies' Generalissimo, France's Marshal Ferdinand Foch, instructed the Allies to take advantage of their numerical strength and superior resources by attacking different parts of the German line little and often, so that Germany would not have time to recover.

The first of these battles was the British-led Allied victory, the Battle of Amiens. Unknown to those involved at the time, it was the beginning of the end of the First World War. **At this stage in the war, the Allies were superior in numbers, equipment and morale.**

On 8th August 1918 at 4.20AM the British attack began. To keep the element of surprise, the preparations were conducted as quietly as possible, and at 5.05AM the French joined the attack. By 7.30AM the Allies had broken through the first German defensive lines. The following day, the Canadian Corps gained another three miles!

The newly formed Royal Air Force (see page 77) were also involved in this battle, attacking bridges behind German lines. This battle was closed on 12th August, and the Allies began preparing for the next.

A Wrecked German Long Range Gun Which Used To Shell Amiens, 1918 by Adrian Hill (1895–1977), a British artist, broadcaster and populariser of art.

THE BREAKING OF THE HINDENBURG LINE

After the success of the Battle of Amiens, Foch proposed a four-stage offensive. This began with an American attack on 26th September 1918 in Meuse-Argonne. The next day, British armies attacked towards Cambrai, and the next day another attack was planned for Flanders. Foch's final stage, on 29th September, was the main assault led by the British and French armies, which focused on breaking through the Germans' fallback defensive position, the Hindenburg Line. **The Germans could not respond to the quick and aggressive attacks. By 5th October the Allies had breached the Hindenburg Line**.

The Allies recaptured towns and cities they had lost throughout the war, and by early November 1918 they recaptured Mons, the city where they had fired the first shots of the war on the Western Front in August 1914.

BATTLE OF VITTORIO VENETO

One of the final battles of the war was on the Italian front and it was fought between Austria-Hungary and Italy. Italy was part of the Triple Alliance in 1914 (see page 8), but switched allegiance and joined the Allies in 1915. **The Battle of Vittorio Veneto started on 24th October 1918 and ended on 4th November with the collapse of the Austro-Hungarian front**. The Italian government and French Generalissimo Foch had been encouraging Italian General Armando Diaz to take advantage of the struggles that the Austro-Hungarian armies were experiencing.

The Allied armies were able to break through the Austrian lines, but the real turning-point came on 27th October, when an Italian officer, Enrico Caviglia, saw an opportunity to cut communications between the Austro-Hungarian armies. The Austro-Hungarian Army could not lead a successful counterattack, and Italian armies were advancing fast. On 30th October, the Italian Army reached Vittorio Veneto and attacked the Austro-Hungarian army. By 3rd November, the Italian troops reached Trento and Trieste. The Armistice was signed at 3.20PM to become effective 24 hours later.

British and Italian troops inspect an abandoned Austro-Hungarian dugout which would have contained up to 83 men.

THE BATTLE OF DOIRAN

The Allies had been fighting in the Salonika region since October 1915 (see page 30). In 1918, French Allied commander General Louis Franchet d'Esperey planned an attack on Bulgarian positions in mountains east of Monastir. French and Serbian troops were successful in their advances.

On 18th September, the British Salonika Force (BSF) began an attack on the Bulgarian forces at Doiran (the Battle of Doiran), supported by the Greek Serres Division and the Greek Cretan Division. Although they were not able to capture the Bulgarian frontline trenches, **on 20th September the Bulgarian forces were forced to retreat and were unable to help other units under attack by French and Serbian forces and the RAF**. On 26th September the Bulgarians admitted defeat, and the Armistice came into effect on 30th September.

The 'Hundred Days' offensive was actually only 95 days long!

HOMECOMING

The Armistice to end the First World War with Germany was signed on 11th November 1918. However, this was merely a ceasefire until the peace had been negotiated and a peace treaty was signed. Transporting people home often caused problems, resulting in many not seeing their loved ones until 1919 or even later. The peace was not properly celebrated until everyone was home and the peace treaty was signed.

PEACE DAY

Negotiations for the Treaty of Versailles took six months, and it was not signed until the end of June 1919 (see page 126). When it became clear that the treaty was going to be signed, attention turned to celebrating victory. A committee was set up to organise a national celebration.

The 19th July 1919 was decided as Peace Day, and 15,000 troops took part in a victory parade in London and there were many more local celebrations across cities, towns and villages. The parade was led by important Allied commanders Pershing (Head of the American Expeditionary Force), Foch (Allied supreme commander) and Haig (British Commander in Chief). **At the end of the parade a monument, the Cenotaph, was unveiled in Whitehall**.

British architect Edwin Lutyens was commissioned by the British Government to design a catafalque – a raised platform to hold a casket or tomb – to be erected on Peace Day. The Cenotaph was dedicated to the losses suffered during the First World War and is now a symbol of remembrance for those who have died in all conflicts since.

A 1919 sketch of the proposed cenotaph 'in situ' with coloured flags, imagined as it would be during a remembrance ceremony with a crowd gathered before it.

RETURNING HOME

For those who returned from the war, adjusting to life at home was often difficult. The war had impacted on them physically and mentally, and life back on the home front was not easy, with unemployment high and demobilisation proving to be complicated.

Plans for demobilisation were discussed as early as 1917, but it was Winston Churchill as War Secretary in January 1919 who introduced the scheme to be implemented. The demobilisation scheme was based on the servicemen's age, length of service and the number of times they had been in battle or wounded. This ensured that the longest-serving servicemen were usually released from service first, but allowance also had to be made for skilled labour to hasten the conversion of war industries back to peacetime production. **In November 1918, the British army consisted of 3.8 million men. The year after it was reduced to 900,000, and by 1922 there were 230,000 men**.

INFLUENZA PANDEMIC

An unusually severe form of influenza broke out in the summer of 1918. It infected around 500 million people and killed an estimated 20 million to 50 million victims worldwide! The war promoted travel for all involved, from labourers to nurses and servicemen. As the virus was extremely contagious, it was carried across the world, infecting and killing more people!

Victims often died within hours of realising they were affected; their skin would turn blue and their lungs would fill up, causing suffocation! The virus disappeared by the summer of 1919, but not before it had claimed more lives than the First World War.

Self-Portrait with the Spanish Flu (1919) by Norwegian painter Edvard Munch (1863–1944).

THE IOLAIRE DISASTER

One of the worst peacetime shipping disasters to befall British coastal waters occurred in the immediate aftermath of the First World War. Built as a luxury yacht in 1881, HMY *Iolaire* was ordered to bring returning servicemen home to the Isle of Lewis in time for the New Year, the first time for four years that some families would be together. However tragedy struck: **in the early hours of New Year's Day 1919, the sailing vessel sank at the entrance of Stornoway Harbour, with the loss of 205 servicemen. There were only 79 survivors**.

Every village in Lewis lost fathers, sons, brothers and the community was left with scores of widows and fatherless children.

DID YOU KNOW...?

THE ORIGINAL CENOTAPH STRUCTURE WAS MADE FROM WOOD AND PLASTER AND INTENDED TO STAY FOR ONLY ONE WEEK. HOWEVER, IT WAS SO POPULAR THAT A PERMANENT REPLACEMENT WAS COMMISSIONED.

'Cenotaph' means 'empty tomb'.

AFTER THE DUST SETTLED

The First World War with Germany came to an end when the Armistice, an agreement to cease the fighting, was signed on 11th November 1918. The wars against Germany's allies were ended in separate armistices, beginning with Bulgaria on 30th September, followed by the Ottoman Empire on 30th October, Austria on 3rd November and Hungary on 13th November. Delegates from 32 countries met in Paris in January 1919 to negotiate a peace treaty that was hoped to 'end all wars'.

The Treaty of Versailles, the peace settlement between Germany and the Allies was finally signed on 28th June 1919 at the Palace of Versailles, France. The treaty included a number of controversial clauses: Germany was forced to admit to full responsibility for the war, pay reparations for damage caused and dissolve her empire.

The League of Nations, an international organisation, was established at the Paris Peace Conference; its primary goal was to maintain world peace by settling disputes before they could turn into war. But 20 years later the world would go to war once again.

The Great War left the world devastated; **more than 65 million men fought, of whom around 9 million were killed**, including 2 million who died of illness and disease; 21.2 million were wounded, and 7.8 million were taken prisoner or missing. Civilian deaths have never been properly calculated. The scale of loss had never been experienced before.

During the war, the poppy was one of the only plants to grow on the battlefields of the Western Front. In Britain and across its former empire, the poppy has become the symbol of those killed in the war.

The Terms of the Armistice by Herbert A Olivier. A view inside a large ornately decorated room in the Palace at Versailles, with senior military personnel and politicians sitting around a large rectangular table.

How are people and society affected after a war has ended?

A NEW SOCIETY

Before the **Representation of the People Act was passed in 1918**, about 60% of men over 21 were able to vote. The Act gave the vote to women over the age of 30 who met a property qualification, and all men over the age of 21. This inclusion almost trebled the number of voters in Britain from 7.7 million to 21.4 million.

Life in Britain changed dramatically during and after the First World War, with previously under-represented groups, namely women and the working class, becoming more vocal and organised. The breakdown in class and gender divisions was spurred on by the role women played during the war and the cross-class experiences of trench warfare.

The Signing of Peace in the Hall of Mirrors, Versailles, 28th June 1919 by William Orpen.

The Wind on the Downs
Marian Allen (1892–1953)

I like to think of you as brown and tall,
As strong and living as you used to be,
In khaki tunic, Sam Brown belt and all,
And standing there and laughing down at me.
Because they tell me, dear, that you are dead,
Because I can no longer see your face,
You have not died, it is not true, instead
You seek adventure some other place.
That you are round about me, I believe;
I hear you laughing as you used to do,
Yet loving all the things I think of you;
And knowing you are happy, should I grieve?
You follow and are watchful where I go;
How should you leave me, having loved me so?

We walked along the towpath, you and I,
Beside the sluggish-moving, still canal;
It seemed impossible that you should die;
I think of you the same and always shall.
We thought of many things and spoke of few,
And life lay all uncertainly before,
And now I walk alone and think of you,
And wonder what new kingdoms you explore.
Over the railway line, across the grass,
While up above the golden wings are spread,
Flying, ever flying overhead,
Here still I see your khaki figure pass,
And when I leave meadow, almost wait,
That you should open first the wooden gate.

DID YOU KNOW...?

IRISH ARTIST WILLIAM ORPEN WAS COMMISSIONED TO RECORD THE PEACE CONFERENCE THROUGH HIS PAINTINGS.

MODERN WAR ART & POETRY

The First World War was commonly referred to as the war to end all wars; unfortunately this was not the case. There have been numerous wars since, many of which are still being fought today. For centuries, artwork and poetry have been used to depict and record the events and feelings evoked during periods of war. Below are some modern reflections and responses to the First World War and modern warfare.

PHILIP LARKIN
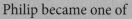

Philip Larkin was born four years after the First World War and his poem 'MCMXIV' ('1914') was inspired by old photographs of men queuing up to join the Army.

Philip became one of England's most famous poets in the late 20th century. He was not a 'war poet', but the fact he wrote this one poem so long after the war had ended shows how the First World War continued to obsess and fascinate people. It has been described as 'a watershed in British history', or a moment that set history and what people believed onto a different course. Perhaps the fact that a famous 'modern' poet felt a drive to write about this war illustrates how deeply and lastingly it is set in our culture.

Caroline de Peyrecave's 2016 portrait of Major James Lyon.

MCMXIV
Philip Larkin (1922–85)

Those long uneven lines
Standing as patiently
As if they were stretched outside
The Oval or Villa Park,
The crowns of hats, the sun
On moustached archaic faces
Grinning as if it were all
An August Bank Holiday lark;

And the shut shops, the bleached
Established names on the sunblinds,
The farthings and sovereigns,
And dark-clothed children at play
Called after kings and queens,
The tin advertisements
For cocoa and twist, and the pubs
Wide-open all day…

Never such innocence,
Never before or since,
As changed itself to past
Without a word – the men
Leaving the gardens tidy,
The thousands of marriages,
Lasting a little while longer:
Never such innocence again.

Cartoonist Ralph Steadman's contemporary response to the First World War commissioned by 14–18NOW.

Rob Heard and the Shrouds of the Somme.

SHROUDS OF THE SOMME

The idea for the artwork behind the shrouds came to artist Rob Heard while he was recovering from a car crash in 2013. He got to thinking about military fatalities in history and how impossible it was to visualise the huge numbers involved. He realised that he needed to 'physicalise the number'. Each of the 72,396 figures in a hand-stitched shroud will represent a British Empire serviceman killed at the Somme who has no known grave. **'Many of these men are laying on the battlefields to this day and in some small way I would like to bring them home. As I create the figures, I cross the names off a list sourced from the Commonwealth War Graves Commission; it's vitally important that each is associated with a name, otherwise the individual gets lost in the numbers.'** Rob plans to complete this enormous challenge in time to display the shrouds in November 2018 to mark the centenary of Armistice Day. 'It will be like nothing else – quarter of a kilometre of bodies laid out in rows, seen by thousands of people, reminding them of those who made the ultimate sacrifice'.

All 72,396 names are listed on the Thiepval Memorial at the Somme. As well as British, these include servicemen from Canada, Australia, New Zealand and South Africa – all countries which were part of the British Empire. The British Empire was later dismantled and replaced by a voluntary organisation of former colonies called the Commonwealth.

To find out more about Shrouds of the Somme, please visit **www.shroudsofthesomme.com**

> How do you think your daily life would change after returning home from serving in a war?

MODERN WAR ART & POETRY

COMBAT STRESS

A number of veterans leave the Armed Forces suffering from mental health conditions. War can cause depression, anxiety and, in some cases, post-traumatic stress disorder (PTSD).

The charity Combat Stress was founded after the First World War to help traumatised veterans cope with their condition through a rehabilitation programme. Almost a century later, Combat Stress has helped more than 100,000 veterans rebuild their lives through specialist treatment and practical support. **Creative expression through art and poetry can be used as an outlet to express feelings of trauma, fear, confusion or loss**. Here is a collection of poetry and artwork exploring the effects of modern warfare produced by British veterans that Combat Stress has helped.

To find out more about Combat Stress, please visit **www.combatstress.org.uk**

Comradeship, or the friendship between men and women who shared the risks of war, is one of the most common themes in war poetry. Men often said that they were fighting, not for their country or for hatred of the enemy, but for their comrades.

I Sit – *Combat Stress Veteran*

I sit and wonder why

Why I sit and cry

Emotions crawling from the deep

Unto the heart

Heart ache for the few left behind

Guilt unable to help brothers in arms

Despair and grief an unhonourable death

Taken for no reason or benefit to anyone

'Meaningless'

I miss you all and long to see you again in the time after.

Remembrance – *Peter Biggs*

Remembrance time to recall

Those who gave all

Soldiers Sailor Airmen

And all that answered the call

Mothers Fathers Lovers

Sons Daughters and Brothers

Sisters Wife's Girlfriends

Boyfriends and all

Whose life we cannot recall

Let's not forget those who

Came back without all

Those brave Boys and Girls

That now face it all in the

Hope to bring peace to us all

Our duty is to remember them all

Those that give freedom to us all.

The idea of 'shell shock' – men whose minds were as wounded by combat as their bodies – was invented in the First World War.

Before that, and earlier in the war, those suffering from combat stress were often simply accused of cowardice.

On That Day – *Ian Warner*

I can remember that day, like it was yesterday
Although the rest of my life seem to be a bit of a haze
The radio crackles and voices come from within
To tell of an accident, not knowing where to begin
Quick lad, a stern voice says to me
Grab all your kit and be as quick as can be
Where are we going, we all seem to ask
Brace yourself lads, this is a horrible task
A Lynx has gone down 16 clicks from here
All of a sudden I came over quite queer
We boarded a chopper as quick as could be
To fly us off to this devastating scene
All I can hear are the cries out loud
Does this explain why I can't cope with crowds?
The distinct smell in the air of aviation fuel
Why is it, that nature has to be so cruel?
Twenty one years on I can still hear the screams
The whole situation comes alive in my dreams
So here I am in the arms of Combat Stress
To try and make sense of this horrible mess
I know deep down I will always remember
But I pray that it won't be my soul I surrender!!!

Combat Stress Veteran - PTSD: Like being a T-Rex... trying to change the bed sheets...

Cases of PTSD were first documented during The First World War when soldiers developed shell shock as a result of the harrowing conditions in the trenches. However, the condition was not officially recognised as a mental health condition until 1980.

How does war impact on our world today?

SOURCES

Adams, Simon.(2014) Eyewitness World War I, Dorling Kindersley World War I London: DK Publishing Inc.

African women in war: World War 1: National Army Museum https://thesamsonsedhistorian.files.wordpress.com/2013/04/african-women-at-war-paper-may-2017.pdf

Alpha History, The Russian Revolution http://alphahistory.com/russianrevolution

Australian War Memorial https://www.awm.gov.au

African Research Institute http://www.africaresearchinstitute.org

Anzacs, Gallipoli and the Anzacs: www.anzacsite.gov.au

Anzac Centenary, Women and the First World War http://anzaccentenary.vic.gov.au/women-first-world-war

BBC Bitesize, Ear of the Great War (Scotland) http://www.bbc.co.uk/education/topics/z8phvcw

BBC iWonder http://www.bbc.co.uk/iwonder

BBC News http://www.bbc.co.uk/news/uk-england-29954113

BBC Wales History http://www.bbc.co.uk/wales/history

BBC, World War One www.bbc.co.uk/history/0/ww1

Black History Month http://www.blackhistorymonth.org.uk/article/section/bhm-heroes/black-history-month-firsts-lilian-bader

Britannica, World War I http://www.britannica.com/event/World-War-I

British Red Cross, Museum and archives http://www.redcross.org.uk/About-us/Who-we-are/Museum-and-archives

Brocklehurst, R. (2007) The Usborne Introduction to the First World War, London: Usborne Publishing Limited

Canadian Soldiers http://www.canadiansoldiers.com

Canadian War Museum http://www.warmuseum.ca/firstworldwar/introduction/key-canadian-events/?anchor=37

Chilvers, I. (ed.) (2009) The Oxford Dictionary of Art and Artists, Oxford: Oxford University Press

Commonwealth of Australia, WWI Gallipoli www.army.gov.au/Our-history/History-in-Focus/WWI-Gallipoli

Commonwealth War Graves Commission www.cwgc.org/

Das, S. (2015) Responses to the War (India), International Encyclopaedia of the First World War

http://encyclopedia.1914—1918-online.net/article/responses_to_the_war_india

Economist, China and the First World War (blog) www.economist.com/blogs/charlemagne/2010/04/china_and_first_world_war

Education Scotland, Impact of the Great War, 1914-1928 http://www.educationscotland.gov.uk/higherscottishhistory/impactofthegreatwar/index.asp

Farquharson-Roberts , M. (2014) A History of the Royal Navy: World War I, London: I B Taurus

First World War www.firstworldwar.com

First World War 1914—18, Australian War Memorial https://www.awm.gov.au/atwar/ww1

Gayford, T. (2014) Black Comedy: cartoons in the First World War http://www.apollo-magazine.com/blackcomedy-cartoons-first-world-war

Glasgow Digital Library, Clydeside rent strikes 1915-16 http://gdl.cdlr.strath.ac.uk/redclyde/redclyeve05.htm

Glasgow University's Great War Project https://glasgowunigreatwar.wordpress.com

Hislop, I. (2013) The Wipers Times: Ian Hislop on the wartime newspaper that laughed in the face of death http://www.radiotimes.com/news/2013-09-11/the-wipers-times-ian-hislop-on-the-wartimenewspaper-that-laughed-in-the-face-of-death

History, World War I www.history.com/topics/world-war-i

History Learning Site, World War One www.historylearningsite.co.uk/world_war_one.htm

Imperial War Museum www.iwm.org.uk

International Encyclopaedia of the First World War http://encyclopedia.1914—1918-online.net/home.html

Isle of Man Government, World War One Commemoration https://www.gov.im/categories/homeand-neighbourhood/world-war-onecommemoration/?iomg-device=Mobile

Jersey Government, WWI Commemoration http://www.jersey.com/english/discoverjersey/aboutjersey/history/Pages/Jersey-WWI-Commemoration.aspx

Kennedy, Rosalind. (2014) The Children's War: Britain, 1914—1918, Palgrave Macmillan Kimmelman, Michael. (2013) In a Rediscovered Trove of Art, a Triumph Over the Nazis' Will, The New York Times. http://www.nytimes.com/2013/11/06

Living Heritage www.parliament.uk/about/livingheritage/transformingsociety/privatelives/yourcountry/overview

Millman, B. (2000) Managing Domestic Dissent in First World War Britain, Abingdon: Routledge

Murray, R. [essay] INTO THE SILENT FUNERAL — the Iolaire Disaster

National Archives, First World War http://www.nationalarchives.gov.uk/first-world-war

National Center for Biotechnology Information https://www.ncbi.nlm.nih.gov/

National Gallery of Australia http://nga.gov.au/dix

New Zealand History https://nzhistory.govt.nz/war/first-world-war

New Zealand at War http://ww100.govt.nz

Ngā Tapuwae https://ngatapuwae.govt.nz/

NHS (2013) 'Post-traumatic stress disorder (PTSD)' www.nhs.uk/conditions/post-traumaticstress-disorder/pages/introduction.aspx

North, J. (2012) An Illustrated Encyclopedia of Uniforms of World War I Wigston: Lorenz Books

Omissi, D. (2011) India and the Western Front http://www.bbc.co.uk/history/worldwars/wwone/india_wwone_01.shtml

20th & 21st Century Migrations, 1900-2000 http://www.ourmigrationstory.org.uk/oms/by-era/1900%E2%80%932000

Parks, E. (1992) Die Aix: God Help Us: The Guernseymen Who Marched Away 1914—1918, Guernsey Museum Monograph

Redford, D. & Grove, P. (2014) The Royal Navy: A History Since 1900, London: I B Taurus

Ronayne, I. (2009) Ours: The Jersey Pals in the First World War, The History Press

Royal Air Force https://www.raf.mod.uk/history

Royal Commission on the Ancient and Historical Monuments of Wales https://rcahmw.gov.uk/home

Royal Museum Greenwich http://www.rmg.co.uk/discover/behind-the-scenes/blog/black-history-month-marcus-bailey-and-battle-jutland

Royal Pavilion, WW1 and the Royal Pavilion http://brightonmuseums.org.uk/royalpavilion/history/ww1-and-the-royal-pavilion/

Science Museum http://www.sciencemuseum.org.uk

Spark Notes, World War I (1914—1918) www.sparknotes.com/history/european/ww1

Spartacus, The First World War www.spartacus.schoolnet.co.uk/FWW.htm

The Anzac Portal http://anzacportal.dva.gov.au/

The Commonwealth Contribution www.ww1commonwealthcontribution.org

The British Library http://www.bl.uk/

The First World War, The Returned and Services League of Australia New South Wales Branch http://rslnsw.org.au/commemoration/heritage/the-first-world-war

The Gazette, Official Public Record https://www.thegazette.co.uk/awards-and-accreditation/notice

The Great War 1914—1918 www.greatwar.co.uk

The use of flights in the African campaign of World War 1: Dr Anne Samson https://thesamsonsedhistorian.files.wordpress.com/2013/04/flight-in-ww1-africa-paper.pdf

The Walter Tull Story www.waltertull.com/

University of Oxford,Commonwealth Cemeteries of World War I ww1centenary.oucs.ox.ac.uk/space-into-place/commonwealth-cemeteries-of-world-war-one

UK Government (2013) 'Commonwealth contribution to First World War to be commemorated' www.gov.uk/government/news/commonwealthcontribution-to-first-world-war-to-be-commemorated

Veterans Affairs Canada www.veterans.gc.ca/eng

Van Emden, Richard. (2012) Boy Soldiers of the Great War: their own stories for the first time, Bloomsbury

War History Online https://www.warhistoryonline.com

West India Committee http://westindiacommittee.org/caribbeansgreatwar

West, M. (1986) Island At War, The remarkable role played by the small Manx nation in the Great War 1914—18, Western Books

World War One Battlefields http://www.ww1battlefields.co.uk/others/vimy.html

World War One, State Library New South Wales https://ww1.sl.nsw.gov.au

1914—1918, The Long, Long Trail www.1914-1918.net

14—18 NOW (Images Page 31, 45, 52) Commissioned by 14—18 NOW, WW1 Centenary Art Commissions, in association the Cartoon Museum and BBC Radio 4. 12 contemporary cartoonists and graphic artists respond to items of news and reportage from 1914, to accompany the radio series, 1914: Day by Day presented by Margaret MacMillan. www.1418now.org.uk

RESOURCES

FICTION

Bullets & Billets	Bruce Bairnsfather
War Game	Michael Foreman
Private Peaceful	Michael Morpurgo
The Best Christmas Present in the World	Michael Morpurgo
War Horse	Michael Morpurgo
The Language of Doves	Rosemary Wells
Road To War: A First World War Girl's Diary	Valerie Wilding

NON-FICTION

Eyewitness World War I	Simon Adams
The Usbourne Introduction to the First World War	Ruth Brocklehurst and Henry Brook
Horrible Histories: Frightful First World War	Terry Deary
The British Soldier of the First World War	Peter Doyle
Animals at War	Isabel George and Rob Lloyd Jones
The Unknown Soldier	Linda Granfield
The First World War: A Very Short Introduction	Michael Howard
Art from the First World War	Imperial War Museum
My First World War	Daniel James
The World War I	Chris McNab
Nursing Through Shot and Shell: A Great War Nurse's Story	Dr Vivien Newman
We Also Served: the Forgotten Women of the First World War	Dr Vivien Newman
World War One: A Very Peculiar History	Jim Pipe
Tommy Rot: WWI Poetry They Didn't Let You Read	John Sadler and Rosie Serdiville
Poems of the First World War: Never Such Innocence	Dr Martin Stephen (ed.)
Women in the First World War	Neil R. Storey and Molly Housego
World War I	H P Willmott

WEBSITES

Bruce Bairnsfather	http://www.brucebairnsfather.org.uk
CWGC Discover 14-18	http://www.cwgc.org/discover1418.aspx
CWGC Forever India	http://www.cwgc.org/foreverindia
Every One Remembered	https://www.everyoneremembered.org
First World War Women	http://www.firstworldwarwomen.co.uk
IWM Learning resources	http://theirpast-yourfuture.org.uk
National Army Museum	http://www.nam.ac.uk/microsites/ww1
Never Such Innocence	www.neversuchinnocence.com
Ours: The Jersey Pals in the First World War	http://www.thejerseypals.com
Spartacus Educational	http://spartacus-educational.com/FWW.htm
We Were There Too: London Jews in the First World War	https://www.jewsfww.london

MCMXIV from *The Complete Poems* by Philip Larkin is published courtesy of Faber and Faber Ltd

INDEX

134

PICTURE CREDITS

P10 (top) © IWM (Art.IWM PST 8365)

P10 (bottom) © IWM (Art.IWM PST 12324)

P11 © IWM, George Kenner

P12 map © IWM Q17139

P12 pic © IWM Q1580, Lieutenant Ernest Brooks

P13 © IWM Art 2676, Richard C. Carline

P15 © IWM Art 3819

P16 © IWM Art 3037

P18 (top) © IWM Art REPRO 000684 6, Muirhead Bone

P18 (bottom) © IWM Art 3035

P19 © IWM (Q 88001)

P20 (top) © IWM Art PST 13171

P20 (bottom) © IWM Art Q 106251

P24 © IWM Q 29559

P25 © IWM Art 1439

P26 © IWM Art 2922

P28 (top) © IWM Art Q7842, Lieutenant John Warwick Brooke

P28 (bottom) © Ministry for Culture and Heritage (Manatū Taonga),

P29 © IWM Art 1151

P30 © Crown copyright 2005—11, Ministry for Culture and Heritage (Manatū Taonga)

P31 © IWM (Q 32064), Ariel Varges

P33 (right) © DACS 2018, Otto Dix

P34 © Война с Германией (War with Germany) by Pavel Filonov, 1914-1915

P36 (top) © IWM (Art.IWM ART 2626)

P36 (bottom) © IWM (Art.IWM ART 4756)

P39 (top) © IWM Art.IWM PST 17130.

P39 (bottom) © The 1918 World Series

P41 (left) © IWM (Art.IWM PST 2761)

P41 (right) © Messines Ridge from Hill by George Edmund Butler

P42 © IWM Art REPRO 000684 42

P43 © IWM ART 3090

P44 © IWM Q 7336

P45 © IWM (ART 17053), George Kenner

P46 © IWM (Art.IWM ART 3070)

P48 © IWM (Q 70561)

P49 (left) © IWM Q 61053.

P49 (right) © IWM Q 51353 Rev H. H. Williams

P50 © IWM HU 58637

P51 (top) © IWM (Art.IWM ART 2473) James McBey

P51 (bottom) Mesopotamia © IWM (Art.IWM ART 2680)

P52 © IWM Art Q34470

P54 (top) © IWM Art 2928, James McBey

P54 (bottom) © IWM (Art.IWM ART 2347)

P56 © IWM Art 4279, Herbert Hiller

P57 © IWM Q 659

P58 © IWM NZH 678. By Henry Armytage Sanders.

P60 (top) Canadian War Museum

P60 (bottom) © IWM (Art.IWM PST 12494)

P64 CWGC Brookwood Military Cemetary, UK

P67 © IWM ART 5930 – Henry Robert Smith

P68 © Volksbund Deutsche Kriegsgräberfürsorge

P69 © Volksbund Deutsche Kriegsgräberfürsorge

P70 (bottom) © Volksbund Deutsche Kriegsgräberfürsorge

p71 (bottom) © Volksbund Deutsche Kriegsgräberfürsorge

P72 (top) © IWM (Art.IWM PST 7806)

P73 Copyright IWM, HU 70114

P74 © IWM Art 3077, F Gordon Crosby

P75 (top) © The Estate of Mrs J.C. Robinson. Cartoon Museum collection

P75 (bottom) © IWM Art 3071, George Horace Davis

P76 With thanks to the Imperial War Museum

P77 © IWM (Art.IWM ART 5103)

P78 © Francis Ledwidge Museum

P80 © IWM Art.IWM ART 2708, David Bomberg

p81 © IWM (HU 121582)

P82 (top) © IWM Art 1460

P82 (bottom) © IWM Art REPRO 000684 59

P83 (top) © IWM Art 2747

P83 (bottom) © IWM Art 2852

P84 © www.firstworldwarwomen.co.uk

P85 © www.firstworldwarwomen.co.uk

P86 (left) © www.firstworldwarwomen.co.uk

P86 (right) © www.firstworldwarwomen.co.uk

P87 (top) © www.firstworldwarwomen.co.uk

P87 (right) © www.firstworldwarwomen.co.uk

P87 (bottom) © www.firstworldwarwomen.co.uk

P89 © IWM (Art.IWM ART 249), Norman Wilkinson

P90 (top) © IWM Art REPRO 000323, W.L. Wyllie (RA)

P90 (bottom) © Art.IWM ART 1311, Philip Connard

P91 © Art.IWM ART 1118, Francis Dodd

P92 © IWM Q_102764.tif

P93 (top) © IWM Art 840, C.R.W. Nevinson

P93 (bottom) © IWM Art SPT 13352

P94 (top) © IWM Art 2004, Randolph Schwabe

P94 (bottom) © IWM Art 4235, Sir John Lavery

P95 (bottom) © IWM ART 2618, Cecil Aldin

P98 © IWM (Q 30965)

P101 © IWM (Q 15064B)

P102 © IWM (Art.IWM PST 5042)

P103 (top) ©Historic England

P103 bottom) ©Historic England

P104 (top) © IWM Art 13544

P104 (bottom) © IWM (HU 52451)

P103 (bottom) © National Portrait Gallery

P107 (top) © IWM (Art.IWM ART 2989)

P107 (bottom) Chris Goddard

P109 © IWM (Art.IWM ART 5188 b), Gertrude Leese

P110 (top right) © 2018 Estate of Barbara Bruce Littlejohn. All rights reserved

P110 (bottom right) © 2018 Estate of Barbara Bruce Littlejohn. All rights reserved

P111 Archie Gilkison, The Reason Why

P112 © IWM (Art.IWM ART 3089)

P113 (bottom) © IWM (Art.IWM ART 323)

P115 © IWM (Q 24440)

P115 © IWM (Art.IWM ART 4744)

P116 FANY archives

P117 © IWM (Art.IWM ART 1015) — J Barnard Davis

P118 (Cavell pic) © IWM (Q 15064B)

P118 (drawing) With thanks to the Cavell Memorabillia of St Mary's Church, Swardeston

P120 (left) © The Royal College of Surgeons of England, Tonks Collection no. 01.

P120 (right) © The Royal College of Surgeons of England, Tonks Collection no. 02.

P121 (top) ©IWM (Art.IWM ART 1918¬)

P122 © Art.IWM ART 960

P123 © IWM (Q 25995)

P124 © Photo IWM (Art.IWM ART 16377 1)

P125 Nasjonalmuseet, Oslo, Norway

P126 © IWM Art 4208, Herbert A. Olivier

P127 © IWM (Art.IWM ART 2856), William Orpen

P128 (top) © National Portrait Gallery, London

P128 (bottom) © Caroline de Peyrecave

P129 © 2018 Ralph Steadman Art Collection

P131 Courtesy Combat Stress